"A thousand messengers point us to the good news of a personal relationship with Christ, but this book contains something precious: the good news of a corporate one. Megan Hill has written a love song for the church, a celebration of the communion of saints in all its present practicality and all its future glory. Her message stirred me to greater love for the fellowship of believers and greater longing for the day when Christ and his bride are at last fully and finally united."

Jen Wilkin, Director of Classes and Curriculum, The Village Church; author, *Women of the Word*; *None Like Him*; and *In His Image*

"This book is positively, intelligently, and helpfully countercultural. It pushes back on our individualism, cynicism, and consumerism and winsomely calls us to invest our lives—indeed find our lives—in something we may be tempted to think is simply not worth the trouble—the local church."

Nancy Guthrie, author, *Even Better than Eden: Nine Ways the Bible's Story Changes Everything about Your Story*

"Megan Hill's love for the church and her Savior shines on every page. She possesses an uncommon gift for engaging illustrations and applications. Her theology of the church is biblical, and her instruction winsome as she clarifies what it means for the church's members to share in each other's gifts and graces. Readers will find themselves thanking God for his gift of 'a place to belong.'"

Charles M. Wingard, Dean of Students and Associate Professor of Pastoral Theology, Reformed Theological Seminary; author, *Help for the New Pastor: Practical Advice for Your First Year of Ministry*

"Megan Hill encourages us to think biblically about the church rather than just experientially or emotionally. This book celebrates our 'blessed belonging' that is our privilege as God's covenant people. It is also an accessible tool to prepare us as his bride as we await our bridegroom's return."

Karen Hodge, Coordinator of Women's Ministries, Presbyterian Church in America; author, *Transformed: Life-taker to Life-giver* and *Life-giving Leadership*

A Place to Belong

A Place
to Belong

LEARNING TO LOVE
THE LOCAL CHURCH

MEGAN HILL

WHEATON, ILLINOIS

Library of Congress Cataloging-in-Publication Data

Names: Hill, Megan, 1978– author.
Title: A place to belong : learning to love the local church / Megan Hill.
Description: Wheaton, Illinois : Crossway, 2020. | Includes bibliographical references and index.
Identifiers: LCCN 2019030351 (print) | LCCN 2019030352 (ebook) | ISBN 9781433563737 (trade paperback) | ISBN 9781433563744 (pdf) | ISBN 9781433563751 (mobi) | ISBN 9781433563768 (epub)
Subjects: LCSH: Church–Biblical teaching. | Bible. Epistles–Criticism, interpretation, etc. | Public worship. | Church attendance.
Classification: LCC BS2545.C5 H55 2020 (print) | LCC BS2545.C5 (ebook) | DDC 250—dc23
LC record available at https://lccn.loc.gov/2019030351
LC ebook record available at https://lccn.loc.gov/2019030352

Crossway is a publishing ministry of Good News Publishers.

VP		30	29	28	27	26	25	24	23	22	21	20
15	14	13	12	11	10	9	8	7	6	5	4	3	2	1

For Brad, Caleb, Nathan, and Evelyn
—children of the covenant—

As you grow, I'm sure you will see that
the church often seems unremarkable.
I pray you will also see that it
is the glory of Christ.

Contents

Introduction

Around the corner from where I live, a house is for sale. In bold green letters the lawn sign reads: "I'm Gorgeous Inside!" The message is surprising. From the street, the house is thoroughly ordinary, even run-down. It's a seventies-era raised ranch with dingy white vinyl siding and a location on a busy road. The roof looks like it lacks the necessary resolve to bear the weight of another winter's snowfall. The circular driveway loops around a weedy patch of grass obviously intended for a fountain but more likely currently concealing ticks. The bushes are too big, the windows are too small, and the backyard is nonexistent.

But the sign encourages me to believe there is something more beautiful—and more valuable—about this seemingly ho-hum house than I can appreciate from the curb.

The local church is a little like that house. At first glance, "the house of God" (Heb. 10:21) is unremarkable: a regular gathering of ordinary people committed to a largely invisible mission. We are young and old, male and female, single and married, unemployed and overworked. None of us is much to look at. We sing slightly off-key, and we can't always clearly articulate the faith we profess. Anyone can see that our diverse personalities, political views, and parenting styles don't easily harmonize, and even our most spiritually mature members sometimes stumble into quarrels, petty jealousies, grumbling,

11

and lethargy. Following worship, bad coffee and awkward moments are served at plastic tables in a damp basement.

But the church has more beauty—and more value—than we can see with physical eyes. Like the Old Testament tabernacle that was covered on the outside with rams' skins and goat hair but ornamented inside with gold and silver, the ordinary-looking church is actually much more than it seems.[1] The Bible proclaims that the church is a radiant bride, a spiritual house made with living stones, a pillar and buttress of the truth, the very body of Christ himself (Eph. 5:27; 1 Pet. 2:5; 1 Tim. 3:15; 1 Cor. 12:27).

We may not immediately realize it from the curb, but this house is gorgeous.

I have had my share of ordinary church experiences. I'm a pastor's wife and a pastor's daughter, but I've been a member of churches where I was neither. I've been a church kid, a youth-group member, a college student, a single woman, a newlywed, a mom. I've attended Sunday school. I've taught Sunday school. I've taken my kids to Sunday school. I've been part of a small church surrounded by cornfields and part of a thousands-of-members church in the city. I've gone to churches where everyone remembers my birthday and churches where I felt like I was always and forever the new girl. I have been loved by people in the church—given casseroles and prayed for and encouraged to use my gifts—and I have sometimes been hurt by people in the church—ignored and misunderstood and intentionally deceived. I know I have hurt a few people myself. I've been impatient with the weak, and I've looked past people who were struggling because I didn't feel like mustering the energy to get involved. The local church doesn't always seem gorgeous.

Perhaps no group is known to meet claims of the church's beauty with more skepticism than the generation just a few years behind me: millennials. Among Christians in their twenties and thirties, narratives of questioning, criticizing, and rejecting the church are common. Seemingly, wandering away from the church is the new road to spiritual maturity and religious credibility. But it's not just young Christians who have grown cold toward the church. People of all generations can struggle to look beyond the church's lackluster appearance. If we are honest, life in the local church sometimes seems ordinary and repetitive. Week after week, we interact with the same people and do the same things together. Over the years, we've been frustrated and disappointed, and we have never seen as much fruit from our worship and work as we would like. In fact, many weeks there seems to be no fruit at all. Maybe we aren't about to leave, but belonging to the local church doesn't always seem like much of a glorious privilege.

So what do we do? When the local church appears utterly unremarkable—insignificant in the eyes of the world and pretty ordinary even in our own—how do we delight in belonging there? And how can we encourage those around us—our children and teenagers, our fellow church members, our newly converted brothers and sisters in Christ, our curious neighbors—that the church is more than it may seem at first glance?

I have taken the thesis of this book from Martyn Lloyd-Jones: "Our greatest need is to recapture the New Testament teaching concerning the Church. If only we could see ourselves in terms of it, we would realize that we are the most privileged people on earth, that there is nothing to be compared with being a Christian and a member of the mystical body of Christ."[2] We may be young or old, newcomer or founding member, leader in the church or teen in the back row, but this is our task: to see the church as God sees the church and then to embrace the privilege of being part of it.

In these pages we'll focus on the New Testament Epistles and the beautiful words those letters use to describe the church (though we'll also see these same truths revealed in the gathered people of God from Genesis to Revelation). Focusing on these terms will help us to clarify what is essential to the value of the local church. Whether your church gathers in America or Azerbaijan, whether it has ten or ten thousand members, whether it hosts dozens of activities or simply meets on Sundays to worship, the same biblical truths should define it, and the same biblical truths will foster your delight in the fundamental loveliness of Christ's gathered people.

When we take seriously what God says about his church, it will shape our experience of belonging there.

We will see from Scripture that the church is the *beloved* (chapter 1) and the *called* (chapter 2). We love the local church because God loves the local church, and we share a common testimony with everyone in the church. Next, we will see that the *church* (chapter 3) exists to worship. When we gather together, week by week, to hear God speak to us and then to speak to him, we are at our highest expression of what it means to be God's assembled people. Then we will consider the way the church is organized by God. The church is a *flock* (chapter 4), receiving care from shepherd elders, and the church is a *body* (chapter 5), requiring the gifts and graces of every member. From there, we will look at how we engage with one another—what the Apostles' Creed calls "the communion of saints." We will learn to see ourselves and one another as the *saints* (chapter 6), *brothers and sisters* (chapter 7), and *gospel partners* (chapter 8). Finally, we'll consider what it means to be the heavenly *multitude* (chapter 9) and take encouragement from the fact that each local church is part of something bigger than itself. In every chapter, we'll discover that the local church is much more than it first appears. We'll consider how this knowledge equips us to pray for one another, to speak to one another, and to live alongside one another. And we'll find that there is nothing to be compared with being a member of the body of Christ.

As I think back over years of Sundays in the pew, I have seen the significance of these truths in my own experience. If I have any maturity in the faith, any authentic spiritual life, any resolve to follow Christ, any experience of his fullness, it is because of the ordinary local church. It is because men of God have been given to me as priceless gifts to preach the word of God for the good of my soul. It is because the members of the church have prayed for me and because its children have noisily added their praises to mine. It is because men and women whom I might not otherwise have met are committing their lives to helping me become like Christ. For four decades now, I have worshiped and worked alongside those for whom Christ died, and I am absolutely convinced that I am more of a Christian in the church than I could ever be alone.[3]

It's worth noting that most of the terms we will consider are given to us (through divine inspiration) by someone who had a very complicated church story. The apostle Paul was a religious kid, but rather than growing up into love for the church, he kicked against it (Phil. 3:5–6). He hated the church, celebrated the death of her first martyr, and used all his energies to strike down Christ's beloved people wherever he could find them (Acts 7:58; 8:1, 3; 9:1–2). Then on his way to persecute the Way, he was waylaid. Christ appeared to him, and the direction of his life forever changed. Overnight, the church's enemy became the church's friend (Acts 9:1–22).

We might expect Paul's church story to be all sunshine and hymn sings from that moment on. But, instead, new church member Paul went on to experience many of the challenges of life in the local church. He was viewed with skepticism by church leaders (Acts 9:26). He suffered personal attacks from false teachers and their disciples (2 Cor. 10:10). He was intentionally misunderstood by other Christians (2 Pet. 3:16). He had disagreements with other Christians (Acts 15:36–40). He was disappointed by other Christians (see 2 Cor. 11:22–29). He sat alone in prison, longing for committed fellow workers but realizing "they all seek their own interests, not those of Jesus Christ" (Phil. 2:21). And—in what may be the saddest verse in all of the Epistles—he recounts, "At my first defense no one came to stand by me, but all deserted me" (2 Tim. 4:16). If anyone knew how disappointing the local church can be, it was the apostle Paul.

And yet. This same Paul is the one who calls the church *beloved* at least a dozen times in his letters. He regularly refers to other Christians as *brothers and sisters*. He doesn't hesitate to address them as *saints*. His writings overflow with tender mentions of particular Christians, with longing to be face-to-face with the churches, with both anxiety and affection for them, and with unflagging optimism for their future glorification. Paul knew that the church is more than it often seems: it is the people of God, the dwelling place of the Spirit, and the fullness of Christ. The truth about the church shaped Paul's experience of the church.

The truth should shape us, too, so that belonging to this ordinary gathering of unremarkable people becomes one of the highest joys and greatest privileges of our lives. In the unassuming assembly of our local churches, Christ manifests his glory. Brothers and sisters, come delight in the church. I know it doesn't look like much from the curb. And I freely admit that it is still being perfected. But the Lord himself tells us: it's beautiful inside.

Please, come in.

1

Beloved

LOVING THE PEOPLE GOD LOVES

Beloved, if God so loved us,
we also ought to love one another.

1 JOHN 4:11

Jim came to our church from prison. Over the decades, his life had taken many turns, but none of them had passed through the door of a gospel-preaching church. Raised by non-Christian parents, snared by sin, and incarcerated as an adult, Jim had never heard a biblical sermon, sung a psalm, or joined his heart to the prayers of God's people. In prison, though, Christ drew Jim to himself through the ministry of a chaplain. As a new believer, Jim spent hours praying and studying the Bible both by himself and in groups of other inmates. Under the chaplain's mentorship, Jim grew in his knowledge of Christ until one day—sentence served—he walked out of prison a truly free man.

And that Sunday he came to church. In the next weeks and months, Jim participated in corporate worship for the first time in his life. He sang heartily and wept freely. He confessed his faith alongside the saints and added his prayers to those of the congregation. His comments during Sunday school revealed a deep biblical knowledge that edified all of us. Over time, he shared meals in people's homes, asked questions, and learned the names of the church's children. He began to greet church members with enthusiastic hugs. On the day that Jim joined our church, he gave his testimony of coming to faith. As he concluded, he looked out over the congregation and reflected with obvious delight, "I've never had a people before."

After he said that, I glanced around the room. Frankly, we weren't much to get excited about. We had just finished a post-worship, bring-a-dish-to-share fellowship lunch, and we sat together at tables littered with crumpled napkins. Listening to Jim's story of coming to Christ, the adults half-heartedly picked at dry remnants of baked ziti on paper plates. The kids, antsy with so much sitting, ran circles around the room or sneaked a third chocolate chip cookie from the dessert table. On the whole, we weren't powerful, rich, intelligent, beautiful, or even especially godly. We were an unassuming collection of graduate students and grandmothers, musicians and mechanics, infants and immigrants. We were just ordinary people who would have to get up on Monday morning and do the next thing. Jim's delight over belonging with us almost seemed naïve.

But Jim wasn't naïve. He was loving what God loves.

God Loves His People

More than thirty times the New Testament writers address the church as "beloved."[1] And as we seek to embrace the privilege of belonging to the local church, we too must begin with this fundamental truth: God loves his people. Toward those who are his own, God has a real heart affection and delight, a settled commitment to sacrificially seek their good, and a desire to see them grow in holiness. We will also see that the local church—*a body of believers and their children in a particular location under the leadership of elders*—is God's beloved, visible people in this world and that we ought to love them as he does.[2] Finally, we will delight in the fact that belonging to the beloved brings us into fellowship with Christ himself.

It's worth noting here that Scripture also attaches the word *beloved* to many of the other terms and truths we'll consider later in this book: Jude encourages the church that they are "called, beloved . . . and kept" (Jude 1), and Paul reminds them that they are both "holy and beloved" (Col. 3:12). The apostolic writers address their readers as "beloved brothers" (e.g., 1 Cor. 15:58; James 1:16); Paul mentions his "beloved fellow worker" (Philem. 1); and John calls the church in eternity "the beloved city" (Rev. 20:9). In future chapters, we'll see that the local church has several glorious identities. We are (among other things) those called in Christ, made saints, joined as brothers and sisters, appointed as partners in gospel work, and included in the heavenly multitude. In this chapter, we'll see that these are only true of us because we are beloved. Before we are anything else as the local church, we are the people God loves.

Of course, God's love for his people didn't begin with your local church, or even with the establishment of the New Testament church in the book of Acts. God's love for his people is eternal. "I have loved you with an everlasting love," the Lord declares (Jer. 31:3; cf. Ps. 103:17). In the councils of eternity— before anything was made and before any human was present to witness it—God set his love on his people. The triune God who is himself love (1 John 4:8) determined to love others. And the rest of the story is the story of God making his love visible.

We get our first look at God's love for his people in the opening chapters of the Bible. During the early days of creation, God prepared an arena to display his love. He illuminated it with light, beautified and sustained it with water and plants, diversified it with animal life. Then at the end of the sixth day, with every star and starling ready to welcome them, God created a man and a woman. In love he created them.[3] In love he called them to worship and work in the place where he set them. In love he gave them the ability and the duty to fill the earth with other worshipers (Gen. 1:28). In love he brought them into his near presence. He was with them, and they were his people. When God lovingly gathered Adam and Eve in the garden, he established the first congregation. And it was very good.

Sadly, the people of God fell into sin. They responded to his love with hatred and rebelled against the one who was their gracious king. They spurned his fellowship and clung to their sin instead. But their rejection of God did not cause God to reject them; instead, it served as an even greater arena to display divine love. Though his people despised him, God did not despise his people. Speaking through the prophet Jeremiah, God calls his people—even his sinful and straying people—"the beloved of my soul" (Jer. 12:7). And, throughout the Old Testament we see God demonstrating his steadfast love for them. God made covenants with his people, entering into a relationship with them.[4] God dwelt among his people, meeting with them in the tabernacle and temple. God spoke to his people, sending Moses and the prophets to proclaim his word to the assembly. God chastised his people, exercising fatherly discipline by handing them over to foreign nations. God redeemed his people from the waters of the flood, from slavery in Egypt, from exile in pagan lands. And God added to his people, giving godly families to Adam and Noah and Abraham and even calling in outsiders like Ruth and Rahab. From Genesis to Malachi, God's gathered people are his beloved.

This doesn't change when we get to the New Testament. There, in the climax of the biblical narrative, God demonstrates his tender care for his beloved people by sending the beloved Son. In the atoning work of Christ, God revealed "the breadth and length and height and depth" of his love for his people (see Eph. 3:17–19). He loved his people from all eternity, and he loved them all the way to the cross. We read of Christ: "Having loved his own who were in the world, he loved them to the end" (John 13:1). By his work on their behalf, Christ cleansed his people from sin, united his people to himself, and secured their relationship with God (see Eph. 1:3–10). And because of this perfect, redeeming work, God gave his beloved people to Christ as Christ's heritage (e.g., Ps. 33:12). Christ came into the world to redeem all of his people and to gather them to himself as the holy object of his divine love.

Though Christ is not physically present with us today, God's love for his people is still on display—in the local church. No sooner had Christ gone up into heaven than his people gathered as local churches. Consider this description from the book of Acts:

> And they devoted themselves to the apostles' teaching and the fellowship, to the breaking of bread and the prayers. . . . And day by day, attending the temple together and breaking bread in their homes, they received their food with glad and generous hearts, praising God and having favor with all the people. And the Lord added to their number day by day those who were being saved. (2:42, 46–47)

Hopefully your own local church isn't much different from that. No matter the century or the location, the followers of

Christ and their families commit themselves to gathering where God has placed them for the purpose of worship and mutual encouragement in submission to God-appointed leadership.[5] Our life together may be simple—"the apostles' teaching and the fellowship . . . the breaking of bread and the prayers" (2:42)—but it testifies to a glorious reality. In the ordinary local church, God makes his love for his people visible. It should be no surprise, then, that the apostolic writers all call the New Testament churches "beloved." In the church God calls us out of the pagan world to gather together before him. In the church he dwells among us by his Spirit, promising to be present with us as we worship (Matt. 18:20; 28:20; cf. Ezek. 37:27). In the church he adds to our number those who are being saved, continuing his faithfulness to all generations. In the church he speaks to us by his word as it is read and preached. And in the church he gives us the sacraments—baptism and the Lord's Supper—as a visible sign and seal that we belong to him.

Ultimately, "beloved" describes the local church because "beloved" describes Christ. Jesus Christ is the one whom the Father "loved . . . before the foundation of the world" (John 17:24). From all eternity, the one who was coequal with the Father and the Spirit was also the object of their mutual love. And we who are "in Christ" are therefore those who have been "blessed . . . in the Beloved" (Eph. 1:1, 6). As the people who were created in Christ, redeemed by Christ, united with Christ, and given to Christ, our identity in the church is inseparably connected to his. If Christ is the beloved, in him we are beloved too.

Last Sunday I sat near Jim as our church received the Lord's Supper. Along with the rest of the congregation, we heard the testimony of God's love for his people: "This is my body, which is for you. . . . This cup is the new covenant in my blood" (1 Cor. 11:24–25). With our eyes we saw the bread broken;

with our hands we held the crumbs and the cup; with our mouths we tasted the sign of God's unfailing covenant. In our outwardly unremarkable act of eating and drinking, God reminded us that we are the beloved people who have been redeemed by the blood of the beloved Son.

Loving the People God Loves

And what God loves, we must love. Paul wrote to the church at Ephesus, "Therefore be imitators of God, as beloved children. And walk in love, as Christ loved us and gave himself up for us, a fragrant offering and sacrifice to God" (Eph. 5:1–2). If we are beloved children, we must walk in Christlike love for his people. Repeatedly in the New Testament, God calls the members of his beloved church to love one another.[6] Love for the church ought to be a fundamental characteristic of our lives. You have a people. They are your local church. And our love ought to mirror God's love in three important ways.

1. *Loving the Unlovely*

Since the fall of Adam, sin has made everyone unlovely. Listen to some of the words that the Bible uses to describe fallen people: enemies (Rom. 5:10), strangers (Eph. 2:12), rebels (Ezek. 20:38), and haters (Rom. 1:30); impure (Eph. 5:5), disobedient (Eph. 2:2), hopeless (Eph. 2:12), and ignorant (Rom. 10:3). Our sin not only makes us repulsive; it rightly places us under God's wrath and displeasure (Eph. 2:3). There is nothing attractive about any of this. But, thankfully, "God shows his love for us in that while we were still sinners, Christ died for us" (Rom. 5:8). When we were unlovely, God loved us. We did nothing to deserve his love, but he loved us anyway. In what might seem like circular reasoning, God explains his love for his people this way: "It was not because you were more in number than any other people that the LORD set his love on you and chose you, for you were the fewest of all peoples, but it is because the LORD loves you" (Deut. 7:7–8). God loves his people because of his own eternal, sovereign, good pleasure and nothing else. His love is "uncaused, un-purchased and unconditional."[7] His love is "uninfluenced."[8] He loves us because he loves us.

So we love God's people simply because God loves them. Hear the words of the apostle John: "Beloved, if God so loved us, we also ought to love one another" (1 John 4:11). God's people are not always lovely. Every one of us can be thoughtless, immature, unkind, foolish, and repeatedly snared by sin. And those are just our obvious failings. We probably don't even know the worst about the people in our church. But God does, and he loves us anyway. When Christ hung on the cross, he died for each particular sin of each particular person the Father had given him. There is no sin of his people yet to be discovered by the Lord and nothing that can disqualify his true children from his love. As we walk in love for the local church, our love models the love of God himself. There was nothing lovely in us that caused God to love us, so we don't wait for God's people to seem attractive in order to love them. If God in his sovereign good pleasure has set his love on these people from eternity past, uniting them to his Son and gathering them into his church, then it is our privilege to love them too.

2. Loving Sacrificially

God loves us because he loves us, and he loves us at great cost to himself. As we have already seen, our sin and rebellion set us against God and put us under his wrath. But because of the great love with which he loved his people, he sacrificed his beloved Son. On that starlit night in Bethlehem, God himself came into the world as a human baby. The Son made his home with us, experiencing all the struggles of life in a fallen world. He obeyed the Father's will, joyfully and perfectly. He took our sins upon him, dying the death we deserved on the cross. Because he loves us, God propitiated his own wrath. He appeased his own judgment. He paid his own penalty. He set himself against his own Son so that he might align himself with us.[9] With great cost and out of a great love, God reconciled his people to himself so that we might enter into a relationship with him.[10]

Our love for the local church, then, must assume this same self-sacrificing character. "By this we know love," writes John, "that [Christ] laid down his life for us, and we ought to lay down our lives for the brothers" (1 John 3:16). Loving God's people requires us to lay down our lives. In the local church, we will regularly give up time, emotional resources, money, respect from the world, physical comfort, and personal preferences. But as John Stott explains, "No-one who has been to the cross and seen God's immeasurable and unmerited love displayed there can go back to a life of selfishness."[11] We will learn more in future chapters about the practical implications of our sacrificial love for the members of Christ's church, but for now we can commit to loving the people God loves, even at great cost to ourselves.

3. Love That Makes Us Lovely

The ultimate result of God's uncaused, sacrificial love is to make the objects of his love lovely. Garry Williams writes, "God does not find people who are beautiful and then decide to love them. Rather, he makes the objects of his love beautiful."[12] The glorious purpose of Christ's incarnation, obedience, death, and resurrection was so that he might "present the church to himself in splendor, without spot or wrinkle or any such thing, that she might be holy and without blemish" (Eph. 5:27). God sets his love on sinful, rebellious, hateful, and ignorant people. And his love changes everything about us. Listen to some of the beautiful words that the Bible uses to describe the people God loves: clean (Heb. 10:22), holy (Eph. 5:27), blameless (Eph. 1:4), faithful (Col. 1:2), chosen (1 Thess. 1:4), and lacking nothing (1 Cor. 1:4–8). Like the prophet Hosea who took a prostitute for a wife, lavished on her gold and silver, nourished her with grain and wine, and dressed her with flax and wool, the Lord tenderly gathers his people to himself and by his love he makes his beloved lovely (Hos. 2:7–8, 14–23; Rom. 9:25–26).

We cannot make anyone lovely—not in the way that God does by removing our sin and imputing Christ's perfect righteousness to us. But our love for one another in the church does produce a sort of radiant loveliness that shines before a watching world. The church father Tertullian famously imagined the Romans marveling at the first-century church, saying, "See, how those Christians love one another!" And Jesus himself makes this point: "By this all people will know that you are my disciples, if you have love for one another" (John 13:35). Though we may be awkward and unremarkable on our own, gathered in the mutual love of the church, we grow in loveliness. Our loveliness blossoms out of the love of God for us and in us, and it is affirmed and magnified and publicly displayed in the love we have for one another. It stands before the watching world as an invitation: come and see God's love displayed.

God's Love in Us

Thankfully, our love for the local church is not a self-produced love. We do not have to manufacture in our own hearts the love necessary to love a profoundly ordinary—and sometimes difficult—group of people whom we did not choose for ourselves. Instead, the God who loved each one of his people puts his love for them in us. John tells us that when we love one another "God abides in us and his love is perfected in us" (1 John 4:12). We look to God for the incentive for our love, we look to God for the example of how to love, and we look to God for the love itself. When the God who is love (1 John 4:8) dwells in us by his Spirit, we have everything we need to love his people.

Belonging to the Beloved

Loving God's beloved people doesn't merely bring us into fellowship with one another; loving God's beloved people also brings us into fellowship with the beloved Son. And it does this in two important ways.

First, in loving the local church, we become like Christ. As Pastor Jeremy Walker explains, "It is like God to love those whom God loves—it is godliness."[13] Do you want to grow in Christlikeness? Come to church and love the people you find there. In fact, our love for the local church is one way that God assures us that we truly belong to Christ. "Whoever loves," writes John, "has been born of God and knows God" (1 John 4:7). If on a Sunday morning you find yourself reaching across the pew to take the hand of someone who is utterly different from you—someone whose manners or politics or gender or age or life's work seems to have nothing to do with your own, be encouraged. If you pray for someone in the hospital or visit someone at her home or rake leaves on an elderly member's lawn, take heart. If a smile rises to your lips when you greet a church member on the sidewalk, rejoice. Seek to grow in your love for God's people, and give thanks to God when you do. These ordinary acts of love for Christ's church are evidence that he is making you like Christ.

But second—and even more precious!—in loving the local church, we experience the presence of Christ. Before going to the cross to redeem his people, Christ prayed for the church.

He asked the Father "that the love with which you have loved me may be in them, and I in them" (John 17:26). In the church, because of the Father's love, Christ is in us. He is among us—leading our worship and attending to our prayers—and he is within us—dwelling in his people by his Spirit.[14] When we are there, week after week, worshiping and working alongside the gathered people of God, we will fellowship with Christ himself. The book of Proverbs tells us that "in a multitude of people is the glory of a king" (14:28), and so it is with Christ. He is love, and his love shines most brightly when it shines in the midst of his redeemed, gathered, beloved people. For all eternity, "My beloved is mine, and I am his" will be the song of the church and her Christ (Song 2:16).

Come, belong to God's beloved.

2

Called

OUR ONE TESTIMONY

There is one body and one Spirit—just as you were called
to the one hope that belongs to your call—one Lord,
one faith, one baptism, one God and Father of all,
who is over all and through all and in all.

EPHESIANS 4:4–6

Several years ago, a small, aging congregation in our Mississippi town shut its doors for the last time, and its members drove a few miles down the road to join our church. In a single Sunday, our congregation grew by half a dozen older women—we called them "the senior sisters"—who immediately proceeded to attend prayer meeting and assemble casseroles with unfailing regularity.[1] Their quilt-covered Bibles were well-thumbed, and their joy in the Lord overflowed in congregational singing. I was instantly charmed by their sweet, sweater-knitting exteriors. I relished their melt-in-the-mouth lemon pound cakes. I admired their spot-less, antique-filled homes. And I wrongly assumed that be-cause these women showed up to church week after week wearing pearls and carrying peppermints in their purses, we had very little in common.

It's true that from the outside, I may never look like the church ladies. I'm unlikely to ever match my purse to my shoes, and I can barely remember to grab my car keys—let alone a handful of peppermints for church kids—on my way out the door on Sunday morning. My ability to make South-ern sweet tea is only passable, and I forgot how to crochet almost as quickly as I learned. But these externals aren't the essence of who I am or who the church ladies are. The fun-damental story of our lives isn't defined in our closets or our kitchens; it's defined in the pages of the Bible and in the work of the Spirit in our hearts. And by that measure, we are very much alike.

The church ladies' lives told a story, and that story was mine as well: one body, one Spirit, one hope, one Lord, one faith, one baptism, one God and Father of all (Eph. 4:4–6). Pearls or peppermints, age or race, gender or socioeconomic status never fundamentally define who we are in the church (Gal. 3:28). Instead, we are defined and united by the single testimony we tell: we are the people God has called. Through-out the New Testament, the members of the local church are identified as those who have been called. We are "called to belong to Jesus Christ" (Rom. 1:6), "called to be saints" (Rom. 1:7; 1 Cor. 1:2), "called into the fellowship of his Son" (1 Cor. 1:9), "called out of darkness," and "[called] into his marvelous light" (1 Pet. 2:9). When we walk into the assembly of God's people on Sunday, we are walking into an assembly of the ones whom God—out of his sovereign good pleasure and eternal love—has called.

One Testimony

I have no memory of the moment of my own calling. Raised by godly parents in the nurture of the church, I didn't pray a salvation prayer or walk an aisle or have a sudden revelation. I don't actually remember a time when I didn't love Christ. My Christian testimony—the story of how I came to faith— is pretty boring. At least, that's what I used to think. As a teenager, I would hear other people's testimonies and shrink a bit lower in my seat. I had no dramatic history of drugs, sex, and rock 'n' roll. I had no moment when everything fell apart and Christ stepped into the wreckage. For years I struggled to see how my story had much in common with other people's. But when I dismissed my own testimony, I failed to appreciate the fact that the same amazing grace saves every wretch—whether she is four or forty years old.

The Bible contains a rich variety of stories of God's calling. God called Abraham out of a pagan family (Gen. 12:1–3; Josh. 24:2), but he called Isaac as a child of the covenant, brought up in the knowledge of the Lord (Gen. 26:2–5). God seized Lot "by the hand," physically overcoming his reluctance and delivering him from imminent destruction (Gen. 19:16), but he called Jacob and Joseph in their dreams (Gen. 28:10–22; 31:11–13; 37:1–11). God called Samuel as a young boy (1 Sam. 3:1–14) and Isaiah as a grown man (Isa. 6:1–13). He called Cornelius while he was praying (Acts 10:30–32). He called Moses while he was at work (Ex. 3:1–6). He called Zacchaeus out of a tree (Luke 19:1–10), and he called Saul while he was walking down the road (Acts 9:1–6). In various times and places and life circumstances, God calls his people.

For all the outward variety in our testimonies, we actually have a common story. The congregational song Psalm 136 highlights this:

> Give thanks to the Lord, for he is good,
>> for his steadfast love endures forever. . . .
> to him who alone does great wonders,
>> for his steadfast love endures forever; . . .
> to him who led his people through the wilderness,
>> for his steadfast love endures forever; . . .
> It is he who remembered us in our low estate,
>> for his steadfast love endures forever;
> and rescued us from our foes,
>> for his steadfast love endures forever. (136:1, 4, 16,
>> 23–24)

The song God's people sang at the dedication of Solomon's temple (2 Chron. 7:3–6) unites the voices of all worshipers to praise God for their one testimony. The verses of the psalm delight in God's work of creation (Ps. 136:4–9), his redemption of Israel from slavery (136:10–16), and his kind provision of the Promised Land (136:17–22). As the singers join the refrain, "his steadfast love endures forever," they together retell their mutual story of God's mercy. They belong to a people who have experienced God's redeeming love and who will go on experiencing it forever. The final section of this psalm parallels and applies the covenant history of Israel to the testimony of each Israelite: The Lord "remembered us in our low estate . . . and rescued us from our foes . . . he who gives food to all flesh" (136:23–25). God created his people from dust, delivered them from sin, and graciously provides for them. His love endures forever. This was the shared story of God's Old Testament people, and it is our story in the local church today.

How did God call you? The Westminster Shorter Catechism defines God's calling this way: "Effectual calling is the work of God's Spirit, whereby, convincing us of our sin and misery, enlightening our minds in the knowledge of Christ, and renewing our wills, he doth persuade and enable us to embrace Jesus Christ, freely offered to us in the gospel."[2] This work of the Spirit is displayed to individual people in individual circumstances. You may have felt him draw you as a young child or after decades of rebellious wandering. You may have come to him in the quiet of your own home or during a public worship service. You may have resisted his call for many years or relaxed into his embrace the first time you heard his word. From around the local church, our stories are each slightly different. We came to Christ sooner or later, alone or in a crowd, with more or less obvious effect. But somewhere along the way, God, by his Spirit, called us. We looked on Christ with Spirit-enabled love, and we trusted him with Spirit-given faith. The details of our testimonies may vary from person to person, but our fundamental story is identical: we were once dead, and now we are alive in Christ.

In the church, we all have one testimony. We are the people God has called.

What We Once Were

I didn't know the senior sisters when they were young. Occasionally when I was leaving my coat in the bedroom of one of their homes, I would examine a black-and-white photograph of a woman in a glamorously tailored dress, and I would slowly realize that this poised beauty was the same woman who had just welcomed me at her door, gripping her walker with blue-veined hands. Before I knew them, these church ladies had a beginning. Once upon a time they were children—newborns, even—with silken skin and downy hair. Once upon a time they studied algebra and turned up the radio when no one else was home. Once upon a time they went to work and played cards with friends and pushed their own infants down the sidewalk in large-wheeled carriages.

And strange as it seems, once upon a time they were dead, enslaved, and condemned.

This is true of every person who now belongs to Christ. And lest we think this wasn't our own situation, the Bible makes it clear that it was. Writing to the members of the local church at Ephesus, Paul says:

> And you were dead in the trespasses and sins in which you once walked, following the course of this world, following the prince of the power of the air, the spirit that is now at work in the sons of disobedience—among whom we all lived in the passions of our flesh, carrying out the desires of the body and the mind, and were by nature children of wrath, *like the rest of mankind*. (Eph. 2:1–3)

Once upon a time, you and I and the church ladies were just like any other sinner. Whether our prevailing sins were terrorism or terrorizing our younger siblings, we nevertheless shook our fist at God as we traveled the road to hell. We failed to worship the Lord, we relished disobedience, and when Satan crooked his little finger, we said, "Yes, Sir." Because of our sin, we spent every day under the righteous wrath of God (Ps. 7:11). This was true of the Ephesians, and it is true of every member of your own local church. None of us were righteous, no, not one (Rom. 3:10).

Most of us would like to forget the foolishness of our past—to shove all evidence of our seventh-grade haircut or our membership in that awkward (and awful!) high school band in a large box. More significantly, we'd also like to forget that we were once "children of wrath" (Eph. 2:3). Left to ourselves, we'd firmly clap the lid on our past unkindness and selfishness and rebellion, on our ignorance and lust and profanity. We'd close the door on our former life as rebels and pagans and turn the key in the lock. Move along. Nothing to see here.

This is exactly what happens all around us every day. In our workplaces and neighborhoods, unregenerate people spend their lives polishing their accomplishments and avoiding their past failures. Your coworkers and neighbors refuse to acknowledge just how sinful their sin is, and so they minimize it with lighthearted banter or excuse it by blaming someone else or rationalize it by comparing themselves to other people. Mostly, though, they just try to ignore it. But passages like Ephesians 2 loudly testify to the truth of who we once were. Paul intended for this sobering description to be read out in the local church because only God's people can understand and admit the terrible truth of our past guilt. Every time someone joins the church, confessing publicly that she is a sinner deserving God's judgment, we are all brought to acknowledge again that this is our testimony too. Every time someone receives the water of baptism, proclaiming her need of cleansing, we can't forget that we needed to be washed too. Every time the bread and wine make their way across the congregation, we all eat and drink with humility, remembering that Christ had to suffer for us too.

Freely acknowledging our past guilt reshapes our understanding of belonging to the church. On the one hand, if we are tempted to pride—if we secretly believe we weren't nearly so wicked as that man in the back row—Ephesians 2 shatters our carefully curated self-image. There is nothing about him that wasn't also true of each of us. On the other hand, if we are tempted to despair—if we secretly believe we can't belong with God's people because of our past sin—Ephesians 2 gives us encouragement. There is nothing about our sin that wasn't also true of every other person in the room. When we gather as a church before a holy God, we gather mutually humbled by the knowledge that every one of us has a past that was very, very bad.

What We Are Now

Thankfully, Ephesians 2 doesn't end with our past guilt. Having looked squarely at our wickedness and rebellion, Paul continues:

> But God, being rich in mercy, because of the great love with which he loved us, even when we were dead in our trespasses, made us alive together with Christ—by grace you have been saved—and raised us up with him and seated us with him in the heavenly places in Christ Jesus. (Eph. 2:4–6)

In his mercy, God called us to himself and united us to the Son. We were dead, but God "made us alive together with Christ," "raised us up with him," and "seated us with him" (2:5–6). Our union with Christ is both *representative*—Christ died in our place and was raised as the firstfruits of our own resurrection—and *experiential*—Christ lives in us and is at work in us to conform our life to the pattern of his.[3] Every Christian who has ever lived is "in Christ Jesus" (2:6). This is our common identity and our common testimony.

When God calls us to Christ, he first justifies us. This means that God forgives our sins for Christ's sake and accepts Christ's righteousness as our own. On the cross, Christ paid the full penalty due for our sins, suffering God's wrath in our place, so that we may be forgiven. On the cross, he also broke the power that sin has over us. No longer are we the powerless subjects of Satan, unable to withstand our own sinful desires; in Christ, we are able to resist sin and pursue holiness. Freed from sin's condemnation and enslavement, and clothed in the righteousness of Christ himself, God brings us into his family—making us his beloved sons and daughters and giving us all the privileges of adopted children.

This, then, is the basis of our new, Spirit-filled life. Because God called us to himself, we know God through Christ, walk in fellowship with him by his Spirit, and wait expectantly for an eternity in his near presence. As new creatures in Christ, the Spirit reorients our desires toward the things that please the Lord and away from the things that once pleased our sinful flesh. And, by the help of the Spirit, we are able to benefit from all the means of grace—the word, the sacraments, and prayer[4]—that God has given us. Maybe, on Sunday mornings, you used to mumble through hymns and sleep through sermons. Now, singing with the congregation brings you to tears, and you feel your heart stirred by the truth the pastor preaches. Maybe you were ignorant of the Bible and rarely (if ever!) prayed. Now your mind often recalls Scripture verses, and you work at prayer even when it's hard. Maybe you once disliked Christians and tried to avoid them whenever possible. Now you visit the church widows on your day off and hate to miss a worship service. What happened? You were dead, but God made you alive. And the same testimony is repeated in a hundred variations throughout the local church. We were each cold toward the things of God, uninterested in his people, and unmoved by worship until God called us. Now, we know by experience the joyful reality of life in Christ.

The One Story That Unifies Us

When the senior sisters first came to our church, we were all a little nervous. An entire congregation, with its own history and habits, had joined our congregation, with just as many firmly established traditions and idiosyncrasies. One Sunday we were distinct. The next Sunday we weren't. Like late-in-life marriage partners, our two independent bodies suddenly found themselves inseparably linked. In the weeks after our union, we each had to make some adjustments. For the sake of the senior sisters, we dusted off a few pages in the hymnal that hadn't been sung in our sanctuary for decades. For our sake, the senior sisters gave up their regular women's circle meeting and humbly sat under Bible teachers who were half their age. They learned to expect monthly fellowship lunches; we learned to expect Jell-O salad.

After a few months, we settled into a comfortable existence together. After a few years, we forgot which of our congregational quirks had come from whom. The only explanation for our remarkable unity is the grace of God. Partly, it was his grace in the moment—answering our prayers and giving each group kindness and patience and gentleness for new challenges. But, mostly, I think it was his grace from all eternity that had united each of us to his Son. As members of Christ, the members of our two churches already had a fundamental unity. And as citizens of Christ's kingdom, we had already forsaken our allegiance to Satan and submitted ourselves to Christ. Our past selves had been crucified with Christ, our present identities were hidden in Christ, and the life we each lived, we lived by faith (Gal. 2:20). This doesn't mean our unity was always effortless, but it does mean that we had everything important in common.

The second half of Ephesians 2 (vv. 11–22) applies the story of our salvation to the theme of reconciliation and unity. God's people were all reconciled to God in the same way: through the cross (Eph. 2:16). We also all continue to have access to God in the same way: through the Spirit (Eph. 2:18). This, then, removes "the dividing wall of hostility" between us and joins us "in one body" (Eph. 2:14, 16). Since we share a common salvation, it unites us to one another in the church. It's often hard to know whether Paul is talking specifically in each verse about our reconciliation to God or our reconciliation to one another, but that may be just the point. The first necessarily produces the second, making them impossible to separate. Christ has killed hostility (2:16) and preached peace (2:17) both vertically and horizontally. Our union to Christ unites us.

When people have been through some significant experience together, it often links their lives from that moment on. Aging veterans stop by the local VFW every week or so because the men sipping beer and shooting pool inside understand what it is like to have been a soldier on a foreign field of battle. Adoptive parents and adopted children gather together for backyard cookouts because only these other families know the sorrow and joy of stitching a new family out of a broken one. Cancer survivors run charity races together, linking arms with fellow-patients who have endured months of poison in their veins and lived long enough to hear the word *remission*. If this kind of solidarity is true of people who share our temporary and earthly experiences, how much more should it be true of those with whom we share the most essential details of our life's story? In the local church we are a gathering of people whom God called. These are the people who—like us—were once dead, enslaved, and condemned and are now alive, freed, and adopted. These are the people who understand what it is like to hate sin, to love Christ, and to strive to be more and more like him. And these, then, are the people with whom our lives are inseparably linked.

What We Will Be

In the years after the senior sisters joined our congregation, their bodies' deterioration accelerated. One by one, they put down their crocheted pot holders and stopped bringing pound cakes to the Bible study. They no longer invited me to come over and sip sweet tea from crystal glasses. They couldn't come out at night to prayer meeting anymore. Some of them moved from their homes into assisted-living facilities. Others packed up decades of memories and went to live near children and grandchildren. Eventually, many of those women made their final move to that home Jesus had gone ahead to prepare for them. At their funerals, the church gathered to grieve and to give thanks.

I had come a long way from my first impression of the church ladies as people utterly different from me. Over hundreds of Sundays praying and worshiping alongside them, I grew to understand that God had called each one of us, and we had the same testimony after all. But their deaths—one by one leaving this world for another—taught me something more. The church ladies and I share a single story, and death doesn't change that. The final earthly breath of each senior sister is exactly what will happen to me too. If the Lord grants me the years, someday, I, too, will lie in a bed at home or in a hospital, and my earthly body will cease to function. Just like the senior sisters, my heart will beat its last, my lungs will exhale, and my earthly life will end. This is frightening to contemplate, but the truth of our shared testimony gives me courage. Never once, in any moment of any one of these women's lives or deaths, did Jesus ever let them go. And just as certainly as he gathered them—and is gathering them—into his near presence, he will bring me by the hand into his glory too. We had a shared story in this life, and we will continue to have a shared story for all eternity.

One day, you and I and the members of our churches will be together with the God who called us. And what will we do when we get there? In part, we will tell our testimony. One day, every creature in heaven and earth—all of those who have been redeemed by Christ—will honor the Lamb who was slain, who by his blood ransomed people for God, ascribing to him blessing and honor and glory and might forever and ever (Rev. 5:9, 12–13). In heaven, we won't tell a hundred or a thousand or a million different testimonies; we will tell a single testimony. We will be the vast multitude in heaven "crying out with a loud voice, 'Salvation belongs to our God who sits on the throne, and to the Lamb!'" (Rev. 7:10). With a single thundering voice we will praise God for our single glorious testimony: We were ransomed by the blood of the Lamb.

The members of your church whom you struggle to identify with may not be its elderly women. Maybe the church's teenagers with their tech-savvy thumbs seem as unlike you as space creatures, or perhaps you find it hard to relate to the academics with their advanced degrees or the blue-color laborers without them. Maybe you feel yourself distant from people who grew up in the church you arrived at so late in life. Or maybe you struggle to see how your "boring" testimony belongs among so many seemingly more amazing ones. But you and they have each been called by God, and "there is one body and one Spirit—just as you were called to the one hope that belongs to your call—one Lord, one faith, one baptism, one God and Father of all, who is over all and through all and in all" (Eph. 4:4). Your testimony and theirs resound together through eternity "to the praise of his glorious grace" (Eph. 1:6).

The local church is an unlikely collection of people, and with earthly eyes it may be hard to see that we belong together. With spiritual ones, however, it is clear. In the church, we all have one testimony.

Come, join the people God has called.

3

Church

WE GATHER TO WORSHIP

And let us consider how to stir up one another to love
and good works, not neglecting to meet together, as is the
habit of some, but encouraging one another, and all
the more as you see the Day drawing near.

HEBREWS 10:24–25

When I come into our church sanctuary early on Sunday, the
room is mostly empty. But as I walk down the aisle, I can see
evidence that other people have already been here. Bibles, notebooks, and tote bags lie on various pews and chairs, placed
there by church members who are now off in other parts of the
building making coffee or meeting with the elders for prayer.
Those personal items mark the seats of the people who usually sit there, and if I think about it for a minute, I can tell you
exactly whose coat or glasses those are, based solely on their
location. I, too, have my usual place, and I lay our family-sized

43

stack of Bibles on the fifth pew on the left before going off to check on the food for the fellowship lunch. I know my seat will be waiting for me when I return.

In every church I've belonged to, from the three thousand–member downtown congregation to the ninety-member church far out in farm country, the members have each had certain places they always sit. We tease one another about our "assigned seats," but none of us really want to move. My seat is the place where people leave notes and return casserole dishes, confident that I will find them. It's also the place my children know to meet me when worship begins. From that particular distance and angle, the preaching sounds exactly as it should, and I've learned to bring a sweater against the ceiling fan's draft. Of course, I may switch seats occasionally because I have a fussy baby or notice a church visitor I want to welcome, but usually the fifth pew on the left just feels right.

Sitting in the same place in church has a long history. In the thirteenth century, churches first began to have permanent seating (prior to that, it was bring your own stool every week). These benches were privately constructed at the expense of individual church members or families and were reserved for their use.[1] If a medieval Christian referred to "my pew," she meant it quite literally. In the centuries following the Reformation, British and American churches installed seating throughout their buildings. These church-owned benches were then rented to members, and "pew-letting" became the primary means of funding the church's operating costs. According to historian Charles Cashdollar, churches determined prices for particular seats according to the perceived desirability of their location—front and aisle seats were the most expensive—but nearly all churches also had free seats available for those who were financially unable to rent.[2]

Eventually, due to changing church finances and concerns about class discrimination, the practice of pew rental declined. Churches replaced pew-letting with today's free-will offering, and members stopped "taking a seat" in church, at least financially. At the turn of the twentieth century, one parish magazine argued against pew rentals, but it also movingly defended sitting in the same place: "If the taking of a seat represents a desire to link oneself definitely to the Church, and is a proclamation that one intends to be a regular worshipper, and so one would wish always to find a place awaiting one, then that is well."[3]

I may not pay a quarterly fee for my spot on the fifth row, but I'm no less committed to being there. My usual pew is not just a thoughtless habit; it's the physical place where I gather with the people of God, affirm my identity as part of the church, and dedicate myself to worship. From this seat—and from every seat in the room—each of us adds our notes to the congregational singing and appends our "Amen" to the public prayers. In our usual spots alongside one another we receive the very word of God and feast on Christ in his Supper. By sitting in those pews for years or even decades, we proclaim our intention to be regular worshipers of God in this local church. And that is well, indeed.

Church Is a Gathering

In this chapter, we'll consider what it means to be "the church," perhaps the most familiar of all the terms in this book. The word *church* in Scripture is the Greek word *ekklesia*. The Bible employs *ekklesia* in a variety of situations to signify a gathering of people, whether organized or spontaneous, for either spiritual or civil purposes. For example, in Acts 19, even the rioting assembly that formed a mob against Paul is called an *ekklesia* (19:32).[4] But the immediately obvious meaning of *ekklesia* in the Bible is a "body of believers in any particular place, associated together in the worship of God."[5] God's people who gathered for worship in Lystra, Iconium, and Antioch, in Corinth and Laodicea were the *ekklesia*—the church (Acts 14:21–23; 2 Cor. 1:1; Col. 4:15–16). And when the people of God "come together as a church" (*ekklesia*), their primary concern has always been worship (1 Cor. 11:18).

Although the New Testament reveals the fullest picture of the church as a worshiping body of believers, it is important to realize that the seeds of the church have existed since creation itself. We noted in chapter 1 that Adam and Eve were not merely the first married couple; they were the first church, created to worship God together. And in the very next generation after Adam, we find an explicit reference to a gathering for worship: "At that time people began to call upon the name of the LORD" (Gen. 4:26). The children of Adam and Eve met to worship God, and their spiritual descendants have continued to worship together ever since.

In the Old Testament, the gathered people of God were the nation-family of Israel, and the central activity of their life together was worship. Theologian Edmund Clowney notes, "The very word *ekklesia* has its Old Testament background in the gathering of the people of God at Sinai to hear God's spoken word."[6] The first four of the Ten Commandments given to Israel regulate worship. They direct whom we worship: God only (Ex. 20:3). They regulate how to worship: according to God's commands, not with human innovation, and in reverence (Ex. 20:4–7). And they prescribe when to worship: on the Sabbath, the one day in seven (Ex. 20:8–11). By his own appointment, God met with his people in the tabernacle and, later, the temple—situating corporate worship at the physical center of their existence together. God also gave them content for their worship—speaking his word to them in the law and through the prophets and teaching them songs for congregational singing in the psalms. God has always prioritized and directed corporate worship for his people.

Jesus, too, worshiped with the church during his earthly life. The one who is himself the object of all true worship sang psalms, benefited from the word as it was read and taught, and joined his "Amen" to the prayers of the people. Even as a twelve-year-old, his great desire was to be "in [his] Father's house," sitting and learning from the word of God in the company of God's people (Luke 2:49). When Jesus took on human flesh—coming as a man to live in particular places among particular people (John 1:11)—he committed to worship. In fact, Jesus's schedule revolved around corporate worship. Luke tells us, "as was his custom, he went to the synagogue on the Sabbath day" (Luke 4:16), and during his days in Jerusalem, Jesus was "teaching daily in the temple" (Luke 19:47). Even in his moment of greatest distress, Jesus joined corporate worship—praying and singing with his assembled disciples immediately before the horror of Calvary (Matt. 26:30). The words of Psalm 122 are first of all Jesus's words: "I was glad when they said to me, 'Let us go to the house of the LORD!'" (122:1). The one who leads the eternal, perfect worship of the heavenly multitude did not exempt himself from the ordinary worship of God's people in the place where he lived.

Emulating Christ's example, his followers gathered for God-directed worship too. In the first chapter of the book of Acts, we read Luke's account of Jesus's post-resurrection ascension into heaven. Before once again taking his place on the rainbow-encircled throne in glory, our Lord encouraged his disciples: "You will be baptized with the Holy Spirit not many days from now" (1:5), and, earlier, he had told them: "I am going away, and I will come to you" (John 14:28). Though Christ was bodily ascending to the Father, he assured them he would be no less present with them by his Spirit. After Christ was lifted up, we read:

> They went up to the upper room where they were staying, Peter and John and James and Andrew, Philip and Thomas, Bartholomew and Matthew, James the son of Alphaeus and Simon the Zealot and Judas the son of James. All these with one accord were devoting themselves to prayer, together with the women and Mary the mother of Jesus, and his brothers. (Acts 1:13–14)

The disciples doubtless missed the companionship of their dear friend and Savior, and they eagerly anticipated the coming of his Spirit. So what did they do? They devoted themselves to worship together. In corporate worship, they followed the example of Jesus and continued fellowship with him—even though he was no longer with them in the flesh. The pattern of those early disciples repeats throughout the New Testament. Paul's missionary journeys are church-planting journeys—in every city, he preached Christ and then organized the new believers as a body of worshipers. Paul's pastoral letters are letters to the local church, frequently containing direction for worship. As the Great Commission unfolded and Christ's disciples multiplied, the church came together and worshiped.

When we come to the book of Revelation, we find a poignant—and instructive—moment from the life of one of Christ's first disciples, the apostle John. John tells us that he "was on the island called Patmos," and "was in the Spirit on the Lord's day" (Rev. 1:9–10). On a day when he was accustomed to joining with the church in corporate worship, the exiled disciple was alone. He didn't waste his island Sunday; he spent it "in the Spirit." We can assume he prayed, meditated on Scripture, and sang praise to the Lord. It was a sweet, Spirit-aided time of private worship, as private worship ought to be—whether we are in prison or walking in the woods. But private worship is never the highest or most glorious worship. So the Lord shows great kindness to John and says to him from the throne of heaven, "Come up here" (Rev. 4:1). Come up here, where you can worship with the angels. Come up here, where you can worship with the countless, gathered people of God. Come up here, where your worship leader is Jesus himself. Come up here, where I am.

We might mistakenly think that we are closest to God when we worship him privately, but John's experience teaches us that as important and intimate as time alone with the Lord may be, it can't be compared to the privilege of corporate worship. As Puritan David Clarkson wrote, "Public worship is to be preferred before private. So it is with the Lord, and so it should be by his people."[7] In our churches today, we should see ourselves as one generation of corporate worshipers with an unbroken heritage extending all the way back to the sixth day of creation. God's people have always been—and will always be—those who worship together. "Come up here," says the Lord. How could we refuse?

Ordinary Worship

Every Sunday I take my place in the fifth row just before the elder rises to give the call to worship. His voice goes out to every pew—to the family with squirming little ones who always sits on the back row and to the man with disabilities who prefers to sit up close where he can best see and hear—and summons us to worship the God who made us and redeemed us. And every week, from our usual places, we proceed to do all the usual things.

In an era that prizes constant change and originality, it can be surprising to realize that corporate worship has neither. We should not presume—God's people have never presumed—

to worship God in the way that seems right to us, whether according to our personal preference or well-meaning concerns for what activities might be helpful to others. Because God is the exalted and holy object of our worship, we acknowledge that he is also its rightful director.[8] As the members of the Westminster Assembly explained it: "The acceptable way of worshipping the true God is instituted by Himself, and so limited to His own revealed will, that He may not be worshipped according to the imaginations and devices of men."[9] When our churches take this seriously, our worship practices will look similar from one week to the next and from one congregation to another. Because we are directed by the unchanging God as we worship him, our worship will also resemble true worship in other ages and places. The same God who directed worship in the first-century church at Corinth by his word directs our worship by his word today.

Summarizing the Bible's teaching about new-covenant worship, the Westminster Assembly goes on to list the God-prescribed elements of worship found in the New Testament:

> Prayer is to be made for things lawful . . . the reading of the Scriptures with godly fear, the sound preaching and conscionable hearing of the Word . . . singing of psalms with grace in the heart; as also, the due administration and worthy receiving of the sacraments instituted by Christ, are all parts of the ordinary religious worship of God.[10]

The first thing we notice about these elements of corporate worship is that they all get their content from God's word. We read God's word aloud, pray prayers based on the promises of God's word, sing songs filled with biblical language and truths, listen to preaching that carefully explains God's word, and see the word made visible in sacraments accompanied by their God-given explanation. From the call to worship to the final benediction, corporate worship is saturated with the word of God for the good of the people of God.

The other thing we notice about this list of worship elements is that it is simple. A worship service that consists of prayer, Bible-reading, preaching, congregational singing, and sacraments will not be outwardly impressive. Instead it will seem quite plain. And if the local church does these things in "ordinary religious worship," it will be doing the same things over and over again. Every time my church meets for worship, I hear a sermon; join my heart to four or more prayers—including a long prayer; listen to at least one substantial Scripture reading and several other shorter ones; sing a handful of psalms and hymns; and regularly receive the sacrament of the Lord's Supper. Multiply that over a year of weekly Sunday morning and evening services, and I annually hear more than a hundred chapters of Scripture, listen to more than a hundred sermons, sing and pray with God's people a few hundred times, and take the bread and wine a dozen or more times. Multiply that further over years or decades or a lifetime, and the number of repetitions is in the thousands or tens of thousands.

Jesus told his disciples that the Father is seeking worshipers to worship "in spirit and truth" (John 4:23), and there is very little in our corporate worship that would appeal to someone who is not filled with the Spirit and not a lover of the truth. Even for those who are, it can sometimes be hard to sustain enthusiasm for a simple worship service just like the thousands that came before it. Worship is a spiritual activity, focused on the truth of God's word. Its elements are outwardly unremarkable, and its effects—the glory of God, the salvation of sinners, the sanctification and comfort of God's people—are largely invisible. To encourage our hearts in this outwardly ordinary practice, we must consider the glorious, but often overlooked, realities of the church's worship.

Your Usual Seat in Heaven

My church's dark wood pews and red cushions are probably thirty or forty years old, approximately as old as the congregation itself. Hymnals and Bibles rest in carpet-padded racks on their backs; small holes cut in the wood hold discarded Communion cups in groups of four.

After years of use, many of the pews sustain scratches, and a few have even come loose from their anchors to the floor. Our pews are familiar, but like the sagging, secondhand sofa in front of my TV, they are not particularly noteworthy.

Over a lifetime I've belonged to churches that had hundred-year-old antique pews and churches that had vinyl-covered stacking chairs, circa 1970. I've also, more than once, been part of a church that was purchasing new seating. In those churches, the building committee would bring an assortment of chairs and single-sized pew segments into the church for members to try. After worship, we'd take turns perching on the samples, arranging our Bibles and notebooks underneath, and standing for imaginary hymn singing. We'd comment on the height and width, note the level of back support, and make suggestions for color and fabric. We weren't going to be paying rent for our pews, but we were nevertheless invested in making sure we had good seats. And for better or worse, future generations of worshipers would owe the details of their usual pew to our preferences.

But whether your church has historically significant pews, custom seating, or metal folding chairs, your seat in church is more than it appears. It's more than the place where you lay your Bible and collect your casserole dishes. It's even more than the place where you regularly worship alongside the ten or hundred or thousand members of your local church. If you belong to Christ, your seat in church is not just a seat in church. It's a seat in heaven.

Hear how the author to the Hebrews describes the church gathered for worship:

> You have come to Mount Zion and to the city of the living God, the heavenly Jerusalem, and to innumerable angels in festal gathering, and to the assembly of the firstborn who are enrolled in heaven, and to God, the judge of all, and to the spirits of the righteous made perfect, and to Jesus, the mediator of a new covenant, and to the sprinkled blood that speaks a better word than the blood of Abel. (Heb. 12:22–24)

Puritan Matthew Henry helpfully divided these verses as "heavenly places" and "heavenly society."[11] We see, first, that worship with the church brings us to a glorious place. The Old Testament temple was doubtless an impressive place to worship—carved cedar walls, altars overlaid with gold, olivewood doors, and basins of burnished bronze (1 Kings 6–7). But the writer of Hebrews tells us that when we come to worship in the local church, we come to a place far more remarkable. We come "to Mount Zion and to the city of the living God, the heavenly Jerusalem" (Heb. 12:22). Worship with the church brings us into heaven itself. Like an embassy building in a foreign nation, whose foundation rests on soil that actually belongs to its mother country, the local church gathered for worship is an outpost of heaven on earth. As citizens of heaven (Phil. 3:20) and subjects of its king, the church can rightly be called a colony of heaven.

Second, we see that worship brings us into glorious company. When we gather with the local church, we gather with those who (as we have seen in previous chapters) are beloved by the Father and share our amazing testimony of salvation unto life. Though they may look ordinary from the outside, the members of our local church have their names written in heaven (Luke 10:20). But when we assemble as the church for worship, it's not only these ordinary and yet extraordinary saints who join us. We join the whole host of heaven. "You have come," writes the author of Hebrews, "to innumerable angels in festal gathering, and to the assembly of the firstborn who are enrolled in heaven . . . to God . . . to the spirits of the righteous made perfect, and to Jesus" (12:22–24).

When I sit in my fifth-row pew, I seldom think about angels. Yet they think a lot about our worship (see 1 Cor. 11:10; 1 Pet. 1:12). In fact, "innumerable angels in festal gathering" join us every Sunday (Heb. 12:22). If the Lord opened our eyes for a single second, we would, like Elisha's servant, be astonished and encouraged by the great company of "those who are with us" (2 Kings 6:16). They delight in the preached word (1 Pet. 1:12), rejoice when sinners repent and believe because of it (Luke 15:7), and testify to the value of even the weakest worshiper of Christ (Matt. 18:10). Commanded by Christ to minister to his beloved children, the angels never miss a worship service (see Ps. 91:11; Heb. 1:14). Not only does our worship gathering welcome the angels; it also includes all the true worshipers of God from every previous age. "The assembly of the firstborn who are enrolled in heaven" and the "spirits of the righteous made perfect" (Heb. 12:23) join us in the familiar seats of our ordinary churches as we offer simple, word-filled worship to the Lord. As those who loved to worship the Lord while they lived on earth, the "righteous made perfect" are a "cloud of witnesses" (Heb. 12:1) in our worship services, testifying to the greatness of the one whom we worship. By faith, they knew him as worthy when they worshiped in chairs and pews like ours, and now they proclaim him as worthy by sight (Heb. 11). When you come into a half-empty sanctuary on a snowy Sunday evening, be encouraged! The gathering may look small and insignificant, but in reality it is filled with those who sinlessly and ceaselessly worship God before his face.

But as encouraging as it is to worship alongside departed saints and heavenly angels, Hebrews 12 offers us even greater encouragement for corporate worship. Not only do innumerable created beings fill our pews, but God himself is there. "God, the judge of all" receives our ordinary, week-by-week worship, and "Jesus, the mediator of a new covenant" perfects our feeble praise (Heb. 12:23–24). We worship God only through the work of Christ our mediator, so Christ himself is necessarily present with us in every service. He promises us that even in a gathering of "two or three"—an assembly so small we might be tempted to cancel the service altogether—he is there (Matt. 18:20). The same Jesus who left his disciples bodily and yet remained with them by his Spirit (John 14:18, 28) shows up for every worship service of those who call on his name. Jesus's atoning work makes our prayers and praises acceptable to God, his presence encourages our weak faith, and his voice leads our songs. Hebrews 2 quotes Jesus as saying, "'I will tell of your name to my brothers: in the midst of the congregation I will sing your praise'" (2:12). However unremarkable and off-key our congregational singing, it is infinitely precious to God because the Son himself is our worship leader, and our voices are strengthened and beautified by his. As the Puritan Jeremiah Burroughs said, "Christ takes us by the hand" and brings us into corporate worship.[12]

Dear Christian, in light of these glorious realities, don't forsake the church's assembly (Heb. 10:24–25). Be there when you are rejoicing (Ps. 122:1). Be there, like Christ himself, when you are facing great trials (Matt. 26:30). Be there when you are tired and when you are doubting. Listen to God's word read and preached, sing the songs that God's people have always sung, join your hearts to prayers that ascend to God's throne, take the bread and wine and witness the water of baptism. There is nowhere else on earth that you will be nearer to heaven.

A few months ago, one of our church mothers had major surgery. An operation that was originally supposed to keep her in the hospital for days kept her there for weeks. One complication led to another, and the doctors were baffled about why her otherwise-healthy body could not seem to recover. Every Sunday, the rest of us came to worship and sadly noted the empty seat on the front right. We sang, but no notes came from her spot; we prayed, but she didn't voice her "Amen"; we received the word read and preached, but she wasn't there to nod her head and murmur her assent; we took the bread and wine, and her portions were left untouched.

Week after week, she wasn't there. And then she was. The elder stood to call the church to worship, and out of the corner of my eye I saw her in her usual spot. She was weak from endless days in a hospital bed and battered from multiple surgeries, but she was there—singing, praying, listening, and receiving. She opened her Bible on her lap and nodded her head as the pastor preached. That Sunday the room felt full again, every person in her place, each of us contributing to the whole. Our ordinary, local church worshiped together, and all of heaven joined us.

Come, take your seat.

4

Flock

RECEIVING CARE FROM A SHEPHERD

So I exhort the elders among you . . . shepherd the flock
of God that is among you.

1 PETER 5:1–2

For the elders of my church, Sunday morning begins early.
While the rest of the congregation is still finishing breakfast
or searching for elusive pairs of children's shoes, the elders are
already at church. They meet in a small room in the back hall
of the building, entering through a door that gets little use on
Sunday mornings. I doubt most people know they are there.
Being human, they often arrive a few minutes late, and some of
them don't come at all, but—largely—they are gathered before
the parking lot fills with cars and the coat room bulges with
snow-flecked winter coats.

Seated in a circle with the door shut, those six or eight men
do something that is outwardly unimpressive: they close their

eyes, bow their heads, and pray. Taking turns leading aloud, they petition the Lord to bless the reading and preaching of his word for the equipping of the saints and the salvation of the elect. They ask him to send his Spirit to compel his people's hearts to sing joyfully and pray fervently. They beg the Lord to show mercy to particular church members who are weak or wandering. They confess their own frailty and plead for grace and wisdom. Before any one of them stands up in the pulpit to read Scripture or preach, before they give a word of encouragement and counsel to a troubled church member, before they welcome a hesitant visitor, they express their dependence on God.

As they close their prayer and open the door, the congregation lays eyes on their elders for the first time that morning. Like many church elders, these men are mostly middle-aged and balding. Monday to Friday they work ordinary jobs at factories and office buildings and government agencies. They have wives and children; some of them have grandchildren. They tell corny jokes. They mow the lawn on Saturday mornings. If you were to see them in line at the grocery store, you wouldn't give them a second glance. And yet—astoundingly, perhaps—these men are Christ's carefully chosen gifts to his church (Eph. 4:8–13).

A Flock Needs a Shepherd

In this chapter, we'll discover the goodness of belonging to the flock of God under the care of Christ-appointed shepherds. It is hard to think of a more familiar biblical image than sheep and shepherds. In fact, shepherding is the first occupation mentioned in the Bible: "Now Abel was a keeper of sheep" (Gen. 4:2). From Abel onward, the pages of the Bible are dotted with wooly animals and their keepers: Abram and Lot owned sheep (Gen. 13:5); Joseph and his brothers pastured their father's sheep (Gen. 37:2); Moses met God in the burning bush while he was tending Jethro's flock (Ex. 3:1); and David was a shepherd before he was a king (1 Sam. 16:11–13).

In addition to its literal examples of sheep and shepherds, the Bible also uses that image as a repeated metaphor for the people of God and those responsible for their care. The most well-known of those passages is probably the beloved Twenty-Third Psalm. There, the psalmist delights in the Lord's abundant care: "The LORD is my shepherd; I shall not want" (23:1). The Old Testament covenant community regularly identified themselves as a flock under the loving shepherding of their covenant God (e.g., Pss. 77:20; 78:52; 80:1; 95:6–7; 100:3; Isa. 40:11). In other places, the metaphor expands to include as shepherds those men God appointed to care for his people. David wasn't only a literal shepherd of four-legged beasts; God called him to "shepherd Jacob his people, Israel his inheritance" (Ps. 78:70–71). Sadly, those human undershepherds often failed the flock. The prophet Ezekiel condemned the religious leaders who ought to have been feeding and protecting the sheep of Israel, but instead "fed themselves" and allowed the sheep to "become a prey" (Ezek. 34:8). Because of the selfish shepherds' failure, God promised to come himself to gather the sheep (34:11) and to give them a perfect shepherd-king who would never neglect the flock (34:23–24). This perfect shepherd, of course, is Jesus.

Preaching to the multitudes, Jesus made a bold declaration: "I am the good shepherd" (John 10:11). His hearers would have understood the meaning of this metaphor, not only because of their agrarian society but because they were looking for the supreme shepherd the Old Testament prophets promised.[1] Here, finally, was the shepherd who would feed the sheep with his own body, quench their thirst with his own Spirit, save their lives by forfeiting his own life, and bring them to dwell safely in his own house. The book of Hebrews calls Jesus "the great shepherd of the sheep," and so he is (13:20). And, in fulfillment of Jeremiah's prophecy that the Lord would replace his people's faithless shepherds with "shepherds over them who will care for them" (Jer. 23:4), Christ the chief shepherd appointed—and continues to appoint—men to care for the flock as his undershepherds. The resurrected Christ commanded Peter three times to feed his sheep (John 21:15–17), making him the first elder in Christ's church. Later, Peter would address the leaders in the churches as his fellow elders and call them to faithfulness in the same work that Christ had given him: feeding and protecting "the flock of God" (1 Pet. 5:1–2).

This quick survey of shepherding imagery in the Bible teaches us a few important things. First, the biblical narrative consistently describes God's people as a flock of sheep. Israel was a flock, and the people who followed Jesus's earthly ministry were a flock, and the early church was a flock, and, likewise, our churches today are also the flock of God. Second, the one thing a flock most desperately needs is a shepherd. "Sheep without a shepherd" (Matt. 9:36) and "sheep that have been scattered" (Ezek. 34:12) are bleak biblical images. There is nothing healthy or safe about individual sheep wandering, unguarded, along the edge of a cliff. A flock needs to be gathered, and it needs to be cared for. It needs a shepherd. Third, the ultimate shepherd of God's people is Christ. He is the good shepherd (John 10:14), the great shepherd (Heb. 13:20), the chief shepherd (1 Pet. 5:4), and the one shepherd (John 10:16). He is the perfect shepherd-king, able completely to nourish and protect his people. Fourth, Christ appoints men to care for the flock in local churches as shepherds under his authority. Like literal shepherds, these elders have the job of caring for each sheep throughout the whole life of the sheep (sheep never outgrow their dependence on the shepherd).[2] In this chapter, and throughout the book, I use the term *elders* to refer to men—including pastors—ordained to spiritual leadership in the church.[3] The elders' responsibilities are primarily spiritual: "We will devote ourselves to prayer and to the ministry of the word" (Acts 6:4), and particular men are appointed in every church to do this (Acts 14:23). Not every gifted individual in the church can be an elder; elders must meet specific, biblical qualifications for their role (1 Tim. 3:1–7; Titus 1:5–9; 1 Pet. 5:1–4). A local church's elders do not rule on their own merits or according to their own designs but as subjects and delegates of Christ the chief shepherd. Fifth—and this is what we will spend the rest of the chapter exploring—the flock's duty and privilege is to joyfully receive the care of its shepherds. Our elders may appear to be painfully ordinary men, but under their loving leadership, we receive the ministry of Christ himself.

Willing to Be Shepherded

The first church that called my husband as pastor was a Presbyterian church in the Deep South. Many of the church's members had walked with Christ for decades, following in the footsteps of parents and grandparents who did the same. Among the people sitting in the pews were those who read serious theology for pleasure and knew their Bibles thoroughly. Over its fifty-year history, the church had been blessed to grow under the preaching of mature men of God who applied the word to their hearts and set an example of godly conduct. The church's elders were wise men who brought deep, experiential knowledge of Christ to the task of shepherding the flock. Because of its location near a seminary, the church had also benefited from teaching by some of the finest theological minds of their generation; seminary professors had regularly filled the pulpit and contributed to the educational ministry of the church. On the whole, the congregation was mature, well-taught, and marked by faithfulness to Christ.

Their new pastor was twenty-five years old.

Newly graduated from seminary and newly married, he came to the church with a sincere love for Christ and no experience as a shepherd. He did some things right. He made a lot of mistakes. He learned to preach, one sermon at a time, Sunday after Sunday. He leaned on the other elders as together they shepherded difficult marriages, wayward children, and church members snared by habitual sin. He grew in his ability to handle the word of truth as he applied it to situations he'd never experienced himself. From the pulpit, in living rooms, and at deathbeds, he pointed people—often people who had been walking with the Lord before he was born—to Christ. In turn, they loved him. Being mature believers, they did not despise him for his youth and inexperience; instead, they gladly received his ministry. They verbally encouraged his preaching, they faithfully prayed for him in their homes and in the church prayer meetings, and they generously supplied his material needs so he could devote himself to daily ministry. They knew he was imperfect—inadequate, even—but they trusted that he was a good gift from the perfect shepherd, so they followed him with joy.

This is the privilege and duty of the flock of God—to receive the shepherding of its elders. But before we can receive their ministry, we must identify as their flock. This means that we must publicly join a local church. Though church membership is often dismissed in contemporary practice, it has always been the practice of God's people to be counted and named. When the Lord redeemed Israel from slavery in Egypt, he recorded their identities in Scripture (see Num. 1–3).[4] When Moses needed assistance to care for the flock of Israel, he appointed men to judge thousands, hundreds, fifties, and tens—specific individuals assigned to specific leaders (Ex. 18:25–27). And Jesus himself defines a true shepherd as someone who knows his particular sheep and whose particular sheep know him (John 10:27). In order for the shepherd to leave the ninety-nine and rescue the one, all one hundred sheep must be clearly identified (Matt. 18:12). The apostle Peter reminds his fellow elders that they have a duty to "those in your charge," the particular people Christ entrusts to their care (1 Pet. 5:3).[5] We are not the flock of God in a general, abstract way. We are particular sheep in a particular section of the flock under particular shepherds. By joining a local church, we submit ourselves to the leadership of those shepherds so they can then know and care for us.

This also means that we take particular care to join a church where the elders meet God's requirements for their life and practice. The qualifications for elders are not a secret (1 Tim. 3:1–7; Titus 1:5–9; 1 Pet. 5:1–5). God gave them publicly to the church, so that believers can wisely recognize those men who are shepherds in the mold of Christ himself. No elder will be perfect this side of heaven, but if a church's elders don't have elders' gifts, they shouldn't serve as elders. Believers should beware of joining a church with unqualified shepherds, but where godly elders seek God's help to lovingly lead God's people, we can happily belong.

Of course, taking church membership vows and being added to the rolls of a local church has implications (and value) beyond identifying the flock for the shepherds. By belonging to a local church, you also allow the other members of the church to identify you as someone for whom they have responsibility. In future chapters, we will explore many of the mutual duties we owe to one another in the local church; formal church membership allows us to define the people who are part of "the household of faith" and therefore especially deserve our care (Gal. 6:10).

Having joined a local church, then, it is our joyful privilege to receive both the public and private ministry of our elders. Acts 5:42 tells us that "every day, in the temple and from house to house, [the apostles] did not cease teaching and preaching that the Christ is Jesus." The undershepherds of the church ministered the word in public—"the temple"—and in private—"house to house." So, too, our elders have both kinds of ministry in the local church. They read, explain, pray, and preach the word from the pulpit on Sundays and at other public meetings of the church. In their regular elders' meetings, they prayerfully direct the ministry of the local church and the wider, connectional church.[6] Our elders also shepherd the sheep from "house to house" as they give personal counsel, answer particular questions, and set an example by their lives. As the flock under their care, we must open our hearts wide to the ministry of our elders (2 Cor. 6:11–13).

In his book for elders, Timothy Witmer describes the fourfold ministry of shepherds: knowing, feeding, guiding, and protecting.[7] As sheep, we should ask ourselves if we are receiving this care willingly. Do you allow yourself to be known by your shepherds, committing yourself as a member of a local church and being transparent with your elders about the concerns of your soul? Do you receive nourishment from your shepherds, eagerly attending to their preaching and teaching, and seeking out their biblical counsel one-on-one? Do you follow the guidance of your shepherds, putting into practice what they teach you from the word and supporting them as they make decisions concerning the life of the church? Finally, do you gladly place yourself under the protection of your shepherds, taking seriously their warnings against sin and false teaching and allowing them to rescue you if you wander into spiritual danger?

The writer to the Hebrews admonishes the local church this way:

Remember your leaders, those who spoke to you the word of God. Consider the outcome of their way of life, and imitate their faith. . . . Obey your leaders and submit to them, for they are keeping watch over your souls, as those who will have to give an account. Let them do this with joy and not with groaning, for that would be of no advantage to you. (Heb. 13:7, 17)

We must not forget that we are sheep under the care of shepherds; we must "remember [our] leaders" (13:7). We ought to pray for them, learn from their teaching, look to their example, submit to their authority, and recognize their enormous responsibility to Christ himself. By doing these things, we will make their shepherding tasks a rewarding and delightful privilege rather than a burden. It makes sense that joyful and willing sheep are a blessing to the shepherd, but the writer to the Hebrews concludes these verses with an unexpected twist. Yes, being a submissive sheep is a blessing to the shepherds, but it is also a blessing to the *sheep*. When we remember our leaders, it is of advantage to *us*! Rather than seeing our shepherds as either forgettable or burdensome, we must begin to see them as a gift.

Shepherds Are a Gift

My favorite services in the life of the local church are ordination services. They are the culmination of what is often a long season—a period when the congregation has heard preaching about biblical eldership, been encouraged to identify men who are gifted for leadership, prayed for those men as they received training and submitted to examinations, and voted to call and ordain particular men to the office of elder. We've studied and prayed and waited and prayed and hoped and prayed some more. The service of ordination, then, is both summit and celebration. We bring plates of cookies and chicken salad–

sandwich triangles, leaving them on paper-covered tables in the fellowship hall for afterward. We welcome members from other nearby churches who have come to rejoice with us. We happily sit, not in our usual pews but anywhere we can find a seat in the packed room.

We sing, we hear Scripture read, and we listen to preaching. The man who has been called as an elder takes certain vows, and the congregation takes vows in response—promising to submit willingly to his Christ-appointed leadership in the church. And then as the new elder kneels at the front of the church, all of the elders lay their hands on his suit-coated shoulders and pray. In the future, this man will go on to pray for the local church hundreds and thousands of times—at elders' meetings, during home visits, from the pulpit, and in that back room early on Sunday mornings—but his work as an elder commences when the church prays for *him*, asking the Lord to shepherd his soul and giving thanks to Christ for his good gift.

Matthew tells us that during Jesus's earthly ministry he traveled widely, preaching in various communities and doing healing miracles there. Surrounded by huge crowds of people, Jesus "had compassion for them, because they were harassed and helpless, like sheep without a shepherd" (Matt. 9:36). The great shepherd looked at the bedraggled flock and was moved. His concern for his sheep then compelled him to do two things. First, he exhorted his disciples to pray for more undershepherds (9:38). Second, he sent out his disciples as undershepherds to rescue "the lost sheep" in the towns and villages, preaching the word and doing good to their souls (10:1–11). In our churches today, we are receiving the answer to the disciples' obedient prayer two thousand years ago. When, Sunday after Sunday, your elders stand in the pulpit and preach the word of God to you, this is because—and only because—the Lord Jesus has had compassion on you.

Nowhere is the kindness of Christ in giving us elders made plainer than in Ephesians 4:

> Therefore it says, "When he [Christ] ascended on high he led a host of captives, and he gave gifts to men." (In saying, "He ascended," what does it mean but that he had also descended into the lower regions, the earth? He who descended is the one who also ascended far above all the heavens, that he might fill all things.) And he gave the apostles, the prophets, the evangelists, the shepherds and teachers, to equip the saints for the work of ministry, for building up the body of Christ, until we all attain to the unity of the faith and of the knowledge of the Son of God, to mature manhood, to the measure of the stature of the fullness of Christ. (4:8–13)

In this passage, we learn what Christ did after his resurrection and ascension into heaven. It's no surprise that the good shepherd didn't cease shepherding simply because he was no longer physically present with the flock. In his absence, he gave them "the apostles, the prophets, the evangelists, the shepherds and teachers" (4:11). Notice how these men are described: they are Christ's gift. No matter how ordinary your elders appear, they are, in reality, Christ's perfectly chosen gift to you. When you receive the ministry of your elders, you receive the ministry of Christ himself. Notice also the abundance of this gift: Christ gave "shepherds and teachers" in the plural. Whereas Christ describes himself as the "one shepherd" (John 10:16), his undershepherds are many. This plurality compensates for elders' human weakness, protects the sheep from any of their self-serving sins, and brings their diverse gifts to benefit the body. Finally, notice the glorious purpose of this gift: so that the church will "attain to the unity of the faith and of the knowledge of the Son of God" (Eph. 4:13). Your elders are given to you for no less purpose than your soul's eternal good. By their ministry, you will know Christ better. We must not discount the privilege of having elders.

Of course, sometimes being shepherded doesn't feel like an obvious gift. When we are caught in sin—like a lamb tangled in a thornbush—our elders will use every God-given tool to extricate us. They will pray for us and offer loving words of concern, but they may also need to "admonish" (1 Thess. 5:12), "warn" (2 Thess. 3:15), snatch (Jude 23), and even "rebuke . . . in the presence of all" (1 Tim. 5:20). Exercised in submission to God's word and within God-established limits, the shepherd's rod and staff (Ps. 23:4) can deliver painful pokes and pulls when the sheep are in imminent spiritual danger. In these times, we should remember the exhortation of the writer to the Hebrews: "All discipline seems painful rather than pleasant, but later it yields the peaceful fruit of righteousness to those who have been trained by it" (Heb. 12:11). The biblical discipline we receive from Christ's undershepherds is "for our good, that we may share in [God's] holiness" (12:10). If our goal is to become more like Christ—and it should be!—we can willingly receive even corrective shepherding as a gift.

A flock receiving the shepherds' care has effects beyond the walls of the church building. When we receive our elders' shepherding and submit to their authority, we display to the world the present reality of Jesus's reign.[8] At this very moment, Jesus sits on the throne of heaven, ruling his kingdom and making intercession for his people. And in the local church this unseen truth becomes visible. Our unbelieving friends and neighbors have no knowledge of what the eternal reign of Christ looks like. None, that is, until the local church gathers down the street. Though Christ's heavenly kingship is invisible, the work of his undershepherds is not. And when God's people submit willingly and joyfully to our elders' loving leadership, we publicly testify to the greater reality of Christ's reign.

What's more, the presence of elders encourages our own hearts. Do you sometimes look at the world around you—its low condition of poverty and racism and false religion, its conflicts and injustices and upheavals—and wonder if Christ is really and truly reigning? Take heart. Your elders stand in your church as an antidote to your doubts. These men are Christ's delegates working to root out those evils in the flock and to promote purity and peace among the sheep. Their earthly rule assures you of Christ's heavenly rule. Just as surely as your elders meet early on Sunday mornings to pray for your soul, King Jesus is continually making intercession for you. And just as surely as your elders use the word to encourage and exhort your local church, King Jesus is ruling his kingdom by the same standard. The whole world will not be revealed as subject to Christ until the last day, but the shepherds' work in the local church points to the truth and goodness of Christ's unbounded reign.

In my church, every ordination service concludes with hugs. First, the current elders welcome the newly ordained man with smiles, tears, and vigorous embraces of the audible, back-slapping variety. Then the congregation gets a turn. We make our way to the front of the church bearing smiles and tears of our own. We reach for our new elder with open-hearted affection, and, one by one, we wrap Christ's gift in our arms.

Come, receive care for your soul.

5

Body

NO UNIMPORTANT PARTS

But as it is, God arranged the members in the body,
each one of them, as he chose.

1 CORINTHIANS 12:18

I can hear the hum even before I open the door. Every Sunday, in the thirty minutes after Sunday school and before morning worship, our congregation talks, drinks coffee, and nibbles muffins at long white tables in the fellowship hall. At first glance, our "fellowship time" appears to be simply an intermission—a chance for people to relax and exchange pleasantries between the main events. But a closer look shows that this half-hour is not a pause in the action at all.

By the coffee urn, two men and a woman discuss an elderly church member who needs to move to a care facility. They agree to ask for volunteers to pack her apartment on Monday. Beside the snack trays, one mom asks another to watch her kids during an upcoming doctor's appointment. At a long table, a church elder captivates a group of children with his sleight-of-hand repertoire, all the while listening intently to their stories about life. In quieter parts of the room, members ask one another for counsel and prayer—some even bow their heads in that moment. Men and women, teens and widows, members and visitors greet one another and express interest in one another's lives; they encourage one another in the faith, and they commit themselves to specific works of service in the coming week. Grocery-store snacks in a pink-carpeted fellowship hall may not sound like a strategic starting point for important ministry, but week after week it is.

Not every church has Sunday morning coffee and muffins, of course. But in my experience, every church has places and times where the congregation enjoys fellowship and draws on the members' various gifts for a common purpose. When I was in Ethiopia, church members gathered on red dirt under the bright sun before the service began. I may not speak Oromo, but hugs and handshakes and deliberate conversations need no translation. In Scotland, I witnessed a tiny congregation share strong tea and quiet discussion following morning worship. In Mississippi, members lingered after evening worship in the vast church sanctuary, migrating from one pew to another with updates, ideas, prayer requests, and plans for ministry. In these moments, the church's unique individuals coalesce, revealing the local church's fundamental identity as a single, interdependent body.

The Sign of God's Blessing

In this chapter, we'll discover the privilege of belonging to the body of Christ. Throughout the New Testament, the image of the church as a body refers to the unity and mutual dependence of its members.[1] The local church is made up of individuals—with particular gifts and varying graces—and those individuals work together under Christ for the common good.[2] Just as your brain and lungs and heart all coordinate and each contributes to your overall health, so every part of Christ's body is necessary for the entire body's well-being. And a living, breathing body is a sign of God's blessing.

Of course, it's not just in the New Testament that we see God's people united for their mutual well-being. Throughout redemptive history, God deliberately gathers his people and then sets them in particular places with particular functions for the good of the whole covenant community. In the early days of the new world, God "took the man [Adam] and put him in the garden of Eden to work it and keep it," gave him Eve as "a helper fit for him," and commanded them together to "be fruitful and multiply and fill the earth and subdue it, and have dominion" (Gen. 1:28; 2:15, 18). Even the very first congregation had unique members who each contributed to the common good.

Later, in the first four chapters of Numbers, we clearly see the individual people of God functioning together under God's direction. In chapter 1, God instructed Moses and Aaron to take a census of "all the congregation of the people of Israel" (1:2). Though we may often be guilty of hurriedly skimming the lists of names in the next verses, they bear witness to the unique members who were each part of God's covenant people. God's appointed census takers recorded the name of each man "from twenty years old and upward" (1:3) according to his tribe. The actual register—with the names of all 603,550 people—must have been impressive. More than half a million people plus their wives and children, each name representing unique gifts and graces, particular interests and skills, and specific life histories.

But the Lord doesn't simply list the individuals and stop there; Numbers 2 goes on to prescribe exactly where each one of those people belonged. Every night and every Sabbath, the journeying people of God made their camp surrounding the tabernacle, the place of God's presence (2:2; see also Num. 9:15–23). It wasn't up to individuals, however, to choose where they might pitch their own tents. Instead, God specifically assigned a location to each tribe. Judah received a place "on the east side toward the sunrise" (2:3); Issachar camped next to Judah, and Zebulun camped southeast of Issachar (2:5–7), and so on. In addition to setting their locations for camp, God also prescribed the order in which each tribe would march out when the cloud lifted from the tabernacle (e.g., 2:9; also Num. 10:11–36). The image we have is of a united and healthy congregation where each member inhabits a divinely appointed place.

When we get to Numbers 3 and 4, we take a closer look at the Levites, the priestly tribe. The census of the Levites was slightly different from that of the other tribes; God commanded Moses and Aaron to record the names of "every male from a month old and upward" (3:15). The presence of tiny babies on the lists reminds us that being a Levite was not a matter of individual decision but of God's sovereign choosing by birth. And to each of the Levites, God gave a particular task associated with worship. The men of Gershon were responsible for the tabernacle's covering, its entrance screens, its hangings, and the cords (3:23, 25–26). The Kohathites cared for the ark and its holy things (3:31), the men of Merari cared for the frames and pillars of the tabernacle (3:36–37), and the sons of Aaron guarded "the sanctuary itself, to protect the people of Israel" (3:38). Each of these families also had a particular place to camp and specific instructions for their duties when the people of God marched out. In order for the people of God to worship him rightly, every one of the twenty-two thousand Levites had to do the exact task God assigned.

This is a picture of God's people as they were meant to be: each individual in his or her God-given place of service, contributing to the good of the whole congregation, so that God's name might be exalted among them. The pattern continued even after the Israelites entered the Promised Land: each fighting man joined the others to conquer the land (Num. 32:29–32), and then God distributed portions of land to each tribe according to his sovereign will (Num. 26:52–56; Josh. 15–21). In the land flowing with milk and honey, God's people worked and worshiped in their particular places for the common good. This was a day that Abraham and Joseph and Moses had longed to see; it was a fulfillment of God's promise and an evidence of God's favor toward his covenant people.

Sadly, following the reign of King David, Israel plummeted into unfaithfulness. One mark of their rebellion was particularly striking: they no longer used their God-given gifts for the common good. Instead, the people of God contributed to one another other's sin. Listen to this indictment from the prophet Isaiah:

> An idol! A craftsman casts it,
>> and a goldsmith overlays it with gold
>> and casts for it silver chains.
> He who is too impoverished for an offering
>> chooses wood that will not rot;
> he seeks out a skillful craftsman
>> to set up an idol that will not move. (Isa. 40:19–20)

Like the architects and laborers of Babel, they leveraged their unity for the purpose of idolatry, so God scattered them into the world. The just punishment for their sin was division and, ultimately, dispersion. In the time of Rehoboam, God judged his people by dividing their one kingdom into two (1 Kings 11:31–39). Even worse, God later sent pagan nations to conquer them, scattering them as exiles to various strange lands. The covenant people who once camped together nightly around the tent of God's presence became homeless wanderers in hostile lands. Scattered among pagan neighbors, they could not perform the divinely appointed acts of service that had once drawn a million hearts to worship. No longer did God's people joyfully gather as a congregation before him—each one exactly in his own place—at the sound of trumpets (Num. 10:3–8); instead, they lived as outcasts, stopping their ears against the cacophony of horns commanding them to bow to a golden image (Dan. 3:5). In Israel's exile, we see the just punishment for sin revealed in all its horror, and we rightly tremble. God's unified people are evidence of his blessing; God's scattered people are evidence of his judgment.

Thankfully, God did not abandon his Old Testament people, and he does not abandon us. He mercifully gathered a remnant from the land of exile, returning them to Jerusalem to rebuild the place of his worship. And in Christ he gathers us in his church to work together for his glory. From the earliest days of the New Testament church, we see a beautiful picture of restored unity and mutual dependence. The believers in the book of Acts "were of one heart and soul" as they shared their possessions, practiced hospitality, fed church widows, exercised evangelistic boldness, and worshiped God together (2:44–46; 4:29, 32; 6:1–3). Each member of the early church contributed to the common good, and the whole congregation flourished.

Throughout redemptive history, unity and mutual dependence among God's covenant people have always been a sign of God's blessing. But in our local churches, we can sometimes overlook this. We are often so eager to see extraordinary

events—growth in numbers or financial abundance or credibility in the larger community—that we fail to delight in the
ordinary breath and heartbeat of the body. When people in the
church encourage one another, teach one another, serve one
another, and pray for one another in dozens of small and large
ways, we ought to rejoice. This is a sign of God-given life and
a mark of his blessing. Every Sunday morning, God displays
his favor toward us in a pink-carpeted fellowship hall over
coffee and muffins.

One Body, Many Members

As we noted earlier, the New Testament often uses the image
of a body to illustrate the church's life of unity and mutual
dependence. In 1 Corinthians 12, in particular, the apostle Paul
highlights three essential characteristics of the church body:

> Now there are varieties of gifts, but the same Spirit; and
> there are varieties of service, but the same Lord; and there
> are varieties of activities, but it is the same God who em-
> powers them all in everyone. To each is given the manifes-
> tation of the Spirit for the common good. . . . All these are
> empowered by one and the same Spirit, who apportions
> to each one individually as he wills. For just as the body
> is one and has many members, and all the members of
> the body, though many, are one body, so it is with Christ.
> (12:4–7, 11–12)

The first thing we see is that the body—just like a physical,
human body—has many parts, and each of those parts has
a different service to perform. As the local church, we have
"varieties of gifts," "varieties of service," and "varieties of
activities" given "to each" (12:4–7). In the last chapter we considered one gift that the Lord has given to his church: elders.
Elders have a specific, authoritative role in the life of the local

church as they care for the spiritual well-being of the flock. But 1 Corinthians 12 shows us that every member of the church ("everyone" 12:6) also has a God-ordained and essential place. Like the Levites who each had a specific responsibility to care for the sanctuary, the priesthood of all believers has a variety of tasks to perform in service to the Lord. In the church we should look for and encourage the gifts of each person, even gifts that are quiet and often inconspicuous. Elderly widows and lanky teenagers each have gifts to contribute.

The second thing we see is that our gifts have been given to us "for the common good" (12:7). Your lungs are useless apart from your body, but when they fulfill their specific function in their proper place, they keep your whole body alive. In the same way, God designed our spiritual gifts to be exercised for the benefit of the whole church. "Having gifts that differ according to the grace given to us," writes Paul, "let us use them" (Rom. 12:6). The person who serves should roll up her sleeves and get to work with a whisk or a mop. The person who can teach ought to sit with the kindergarteners or the senior citizens and teach. The person who has been blessed with material wealth should share it with the father of four who has just been laid off. The person with a merciful heart must cheerfully show compassion for single moms and cancer patients in the congregation (see Rom. 12:6–8). Separated from the body our spiritual gifts are useless, but in the local church they find their proper expression.

The final thing we see is that the body—just like a physical, human body—is unified. In the church, all our gifts have a common source. They come from "the same Spirit," "the same Lord," and "the same God" (1 Cor. 12:4–6). The triune, covenant God who sovereignly appointed certain Israelites to serve as soldiers and others to serve in the tabernacle appoints our gifts today "as he wills" (1 Cor. 12:11). Although our gifts may seem wildly diverse—one person serves the body by cleaning bathrooms, another by preaching sermons—they are unified by the Lord, who empowers them. Our gifts come from him, their use is directed by him, and their fruit brings glory to him. In Christ we are one body.

No Unimportant Parts

Every few months, my church gathers in the fellowship hall for a slightly different purpose: lunch. Each person brings a dish of their choice in addition to contributing items such as drinks or bread from a sign-up list. After morning worship, the pastor gives public thanks for the food, we all file into the hallway, and we wait our turn to fill paper plates at the laden tables. The routine is familiar. The actual menu is unpredictable. Some weeks, it seems like everyone decides to make a pasta-themed dish, and our plates pile with zitis and spaghettis in binary red and white. Other weeks, in an unplanned act of synchronized health-consciousness, the salads take over space typically reserved for desserts. Usually, it's just the reverse. Only rarely do we manage a perfectly balanced table, with veggies and meats in proportions that would make a nutritionist—or mother— proud. When it comes to fellowship lunch, you never know what you might eat. But you certainly won't leave hungry.

The membership of the local church can feel a bit like the unpredictable offerings at a fellowship lunch. Our congregation's gifts don't always fit into a tidy organizational chart or appear to be evenly distributed. Sometimes the church has dozens of teachers; often it has few. Sometimes it has people who are able to give abundantly; often its members are just scraping by. It may have twenty nursery volunteers to every person who wants to do evangelism or twenty would-be organizers to every one who is willing to make the coffee. Often it seems like a handful of people have all the gifts, and the rest of us barely have any. You never know what you might find on the buffet table of church-member gifts.

Thankfully, the particular composition of the church doesn't depend on us. Continuing the image of the church as a body, Paul writes, "But as it is, God arranged the members in the body, each one of them, as he chose" (1 Cor. 12:18). The truth of 1 Corinthians 12 is that however it might appear, the people and gifts represented in our local church are exactly the people and gifts we need. A few verses later, Paul flatly dismisses any suggestion that some people or gifts are more necessary for the body's well-being than others: "The eye cannot say to the hand, 'I have no need of you,' nor again the head to the feet, 'I have no need of you.' On the contrary, the parts of the body that seem to be weaker are indispensable" (12:21–22). Again he affirms, "*God* has . . . composed the body" (12:24). This truth should give you confidence: your particular gifts have a valuable, God-appointed place. It should also humble you: your particular gifts are simply one part of the body, and you desperately need other people with their particular gifts (see Rom. 12:3). Finally, this truth should increase your love for the local church: the gifts in the body are exactly what God knows your congregation needs. Because of God's sovereign choosing, no part is missing, and every part is valuable.

In the New Testament we read five different lists of spiritual gifts (Rom. 12:6–8; 1 Cor. 12:8–10, 28–30; Eph. 4:7–11; 1 Pet. 4:7–11). They name gifts such as faith, healing, prophesy, teaching, service, and mercy, but each list—even each of the two lists in 1 Corinthians 12—is strikingly distinctive. Particular gifts repeat, while others show up on one list and disappear from another. Some of the listed gifts are unique to the apostolic age, and others continue to the present day. We immediately recognize many of the gifts, but we don't even know how to define a few of them. Ultimately, any attempt to rigidly identify and neatly categorize a precise list of spiritual gifts will end in frustration. This is intentional. Peter and Paul don't give us a neat graphic or a quick diagnostic survey, because a mechanical approach to spiritual gifts would miss the larger point: the Spirit gives exactly the right gifts in exactly the right measure at exactly the right time to exactly the right people for the well-being of the local church.[3] As we look around our church, we can trust that the assembled gifts, whatever they are, are for our good.

The Fullness of Christ

The end of our weekly fellowship time always seems to arrive quickly. As the clock ticks toward ten-thirty and the beginning of worship, someone flashes the lights in the fellowship hall. Called to attention, mothers gather children, devoted coffee drinkers drain their cups, and the teens jostle good-naturedly on their way to the door. The pastor scribbles one more thought on his sermon notes while a young man silently cleans the inevitable crumbs from tables and chairs. We might not set foot in this room until next Sunday, but we leave committed to using our gifts in the coming days; we'll meet later in the week to unload boxes at the nursing home or to visit the sick or to pray for particular needs. We walk out the door with a renewed sense of our own God-assigned place and our own God-given duties. But we also leave with something more. As I turn my head to look back over the quickly emptying fellowship hall, I realize that in this simple half-hour gathering, we have enjoyed Christ himself.

At the very beginning of his discussion of spiritual gifts in 1 Corinthians 12, Paul clarifies that the ultimate goal of all spiritual gifts is to bring glory to Christ. Paul writes, "No one speaking in the Spirit of God ever says 'Jesus is accursed!' and no one can say 'Jesus is Lord' except in the Holy Spirit" (12:3).

81

Any gifts that God's people have from the Spirit are given so that Christ will be exalted.[4] Like the gifts of the Old Testament Levites, which were each assigned to together facilitate the true worship of God, our gifts—whether mentoring teens or assembling casseroles—coordinate with the gifts of the whole congregation to magnify the name of Christ. When one person prays in his heart for the sermon, a second person encourages children to listen, a third person preaches, and a fourth person collects trash after the service is over, we each contribute to Christ's exaltation in our midst.

But there's more. In the first chapter of Ephesians, we read an amazing description of the church: "And [God] put all things under [Christ's] feet and gave him as head over all things to the church, which is his body, the fullness of him who fills all in all" (1:22–23). In the church, Paul writes, Christ fills us with his fullness. In the church, then, we see our Savior. God gives each believer the Spirit in some measure ("according to the measure of faith that God has assigned," Rom. 12:3), but God gave Christ the Spirit "without measure" (John 3:34).[5] We each have some gifts. Christ has all the gifts. We each serve in some ways. Christ serves in every way. A few of us have wisdom, a few have gifts of mercy, and a few are able to teach and exhort. Christ has "all the treasures of wisdom and knowledge" (Col. 2:3), extends mercy perfectly and effectively, and is the Word made flesh (John 1:14). As Matthew Henry writes, "Jesus Christ filleth all in all; he supplies all defects in all his members, filling them with his Spirit, and even with the fulness [*sic*] of God."[6] On her own, each believer reflects Christ in a small way, but together as the church, we know the fullness of Christ who fill us.

Astoundingly, there's even more. Not only does Christ fill the church, but the church is the fullness of Christ.[7] Christ cannot be a head without a body; he cannot be a king without a kingdom; he cannot be a mediator without his people; he cannot be a redeemer without his church. The Father validated the work of Christ by raising him from the dead, seating him on the throne, and giving him a body (Eph. 1:20–23). The church is the irrefutable evidence of Christ's complete and effective atonement for his people. The fact that we use our diverse gifts not for selfish gain but for one another's good testifies to Christ's reconciling work. The fact that every part inhabits a particular and valuable place affirms Christ's rightful identity as our divine head. Throughout the world, and even in the presence of "rulers and authorities in the heavenly places," the existence of the church boldly proclaims the truth of the gospel (Eph. 3:10). In our unity and our mutual dependence as we worship and work together, we display Christ himself.

Dear Christian, do you want to experience the fullness of Christ? Belong to the church. Use your gifts where he sets you. Exhort. Serve. Give. Show mercy. Work alongside his people for the common good. Then—in the unassuming surroundings of the fellowship hall or the church basement or the aisles between the pews—you will know firsthand the fullness of Christ. In fact, you cannot experience it in any other way.

Come, take your place.

6

Saints

HOLINESS IS A COMMUNITY PROJECT

... to those sanctified in Christ Jesus, called to be saints
together with all those who in every place call upon the
name of our Lord Jesus Christ, both their Lord and ours.

1 CORINTHIANS 1:2

Every six months, our family spends a Saturday morning at the
church. We gulp down our breakfasts, lace up our sneakers,
and tug on worn sweatshirts. We arrive at the church sleepy-
eyed and bed-headed. We are not attending a church event.
In fact, we are usually the only people in the building. We are
there to clean.

Alongside our kids, my husband and I walk down the back
hallway and open the door to the cleaning closet. Someone
has taped a checklist to the wall for the benefit of each week's
assigned cleaners: Dust pews. Empty garbage cans. Clean sinks
and toilets in bathrooms. Mop bathroom floors. Collect and

dispose of old bulletins, Communion cups, and other trash. Wipe glass doors. Wipe Communion table. After a brief family huddle around the list, we grab buckets and rags and spread out over the building, each person taking responsibility for a particular task.

Usually, I head for the bathrooms with a spray bottle and a roll of paper towels, and it's there, under the glare of a fluorescent bulb, that the combined grime of a hundred church members spreads out before me. Fingerprints smear the faucets, dirt rings the sink bowls, crumpled paper towels overflow from the trash cans, and the toilets are far from gleaming. I notice footprints on the linoleum and a gooey trail of soap on the counter. I'm sure the people of my church try to keep things clean, but our dirt has a way of adding up over the course of a week. I pull on rubber gloves and get to work.

Cleaning the church is not particularly convenient. No matter which Saturday cleanings fall to our family, we always have something else we could be doing. Grocery shopping, basketball practice, cooking, exercise, even cleaning our own house are all put on hold for the morning. Instead of tending to our own needs or interests, we spend hours at the church picking up after other people. It's not convenient, and it's not glamorous. Soon after we arrive, I'm on my hands and knees, using a sponge to clean around the base of the toilets. My hair is a mess, my shirt-sleeves are damp, and I smell like bleach. What's more, it's doubtful that even one other person will pause after worship tomorrow to admire my spotless grout.

But this is vital work. If our family didn't make the effort to clean, the already significant dirt would accumulate for another week. If next week's assigned cleaners also shrugged it off, we'd begin to notice. Eventually, the overflowing trash would cover the bathroom floors entirely. The sticky soap residue would harden in weekly layers. Our unwiped drips and splatters would multiply and begin to host colonies of mold. It wouldn't take long before the neglected church building would become derelict—entirely unusable for the congregation's work and worship. From this perspective, an occasional Saturday morning with a mop looks extremely important.

Of course, thoughtlessly discarded candy wrappers are only a small part of our problem as a church. Gossip, unkindness, lust, greed, pride, partiality, anger, idolatry, and selfishness also pollute the covenant community. They spread and multiply like mold, corrupting everything they touch. If we do not persistently address our personal and corporate sins, they will overwhelm us. Thankfully, the local church is an essential part of the solution. Throughout Scripture God calls his gathered people to be holy, and throughout Scripture he uses them to promote one another's holiness. In this chapter, we'll consider the privilege of belonging to the saints—the holy ones. We'll see what it means to be holy as the church. We'll discuss five ways the local church is designed for our holiness. And finally we'll delight in the ultimate goal of the church's holiness. Dear saints, "holiness is a community project."[1]

Called to Be Saints

Paul begins his letter to the Corinthian church by addressing them as "those sanctified in Christ Jesus, called to be saints together with all those who in every place call upon the name of our Lord Jesus Christ" (1 Cor. 1:2). The members of this church were saints. They were holy: set apart by God, united to Christ, and called to a life of righteousness. As we read further in the letter to Corinth, this designation might seem grossly inappropriate. The subsequent chapters reveal a church riddled with division, sexual sin, idolatry, false teaching, gossip, and disorder. Arguably the most immature church in the New Testament, the Corinthian congregation caused Paul "affliction and anguish" (2 Cor. 2:4). And yet he calls them "saints."

Like the church at Corinth, our local church may be plagued with faults and weaknesses, but it is not defined by them. We, too, are set apart by a holy God from the first moment of our new birth. The writer of Hebrews tells us that "by a single offering he [Christ] has perfected for all time those who are being sanctified" (Heb. 10:14). When Christ died for sin, he secured our freedom from sin's power and guilt. When Christ was raised, he secured our new, Spirit-filled life. When we look to him in faith, we receive all his benefits.[2] On the day we first believe, we are holy.

We are holy, and we are also becoming holy. Paul calls the Corinthians "saints," and this forms the basis for all the other instructions he writes to them. You are holy, he says; now here's what that means for your life. The word *sanctification* most often means the process of being gradually conformed by the Spirit in our minds, hearts, and actions to the will of the Father and to the image of Christ. When Paul says that "we all, with unveiled face, beholding the glory of the Lord, are being transformed into the same image from one degree of glory to another" (2 Cor. 3:18), he is talking about our gradual advancement in holiness. Holiness should have a progressive and active dimension in our daily life.[3] We pursue holiness not to earn our salvation—as if we could!—but because our salvation compels us to live out our new identity in Christ. It is because we have "been raised with Christ" and our "life is hidden with Christ" that we "put to death" our former sin habits (Col. 3:1, 3, 5–10). It is because we are "the saints in Christ Jesus" that we seek to "abound more and more" in love and grow in "knowledge and all discernment" so we might be "pure and blameless for the day of Christ" (Phil. 1:1, 9–10). In this light, our sins are not something to be expected, and they are not something to be tolerated. As saints, we hate our sins and seek daily to kill them because they are directly contrary to who God has made us to be.[4]

What's more, our holiness is not merely personal. It is also the foundation of our corporate identity as the church. The surprising thing about the Bible's testimony is that the word *saints* does not single out exemplary church members, or church members whose gifts and graces are only of a particular variety. In fact, in biblical terms, there are no individual saints.[5] In its sixty appearances in the New Testament, the word is always plural and always used as a description of all the Christians in the church. The corporate people of God are, for example, "the saints at Jerusalem" (Rom. 15:26), "the saints who are in Ephesus" (Eph. 1:1), "the saints in Christ Jesus who are at Philippi" (Phil. 1:1) and "the saints who are in the whole of Achaia" (2 Cor. 1:1). We are not lone saints, haloed marble statues standing aloof on separate hills; we are corporate saints, members of a holy company, and most truly the holy ones only when we are viewed together.

The pews—or benches or chairs—of every church in every age in every part of the world are filled with people in different stages of spiritual maturity. We worship with people whose Bibles are tattered with use and people who still need help to find the Minor Prophets. We join our prayers with people who have been praying fervently for a lifetime and people who are just learning to pray. We sing alongside people who know every hymn by heart and people who are singing them for the first time. We sit under preaching with occasional doubters and with founding church members and with spiritual newborns hungry for food. But our fundamental identity is that we are holy. The saints are the church. The saints are *us*.

Holiness Is a Community Project

Next to the checklist of chores in the church closet is another sheet of paper. This one is a cleaning calendar, with every Saturday assigned to a different family or individual in the church. Sometimes when I'm picking up other people's soggy tissues and gum wrappers and forgotten Communion cups, I think about that calendar. This week it's my turn to serve the church by taking out trash I didn't discard and cleaning up messes I didn't make. Next week, though, someone else will be cleaning up *my* muddy footprints and water bottle spills. Someone else will be giving up her Saturday morning to make sure my dust and dirt don't overwhelm the church. When I'm tempted to be frustrated by time-consuming cracker crumbs in the nursery and scattered pens in the pews, I remember that keeping the church clean is a community project. To address our sin, we need each other.

It has always been this way for God's people. When we read through the book of Leviticus, for example, nearly every page confronts us with detailed attention to community cleanness. The book begins with precise instructions for sacrifices of various kinds: who can offer them, who can partake of them, and how the sacrifice should be conducted (Lev. 1–9). Every day at the tabernacle, the Israelites saw and heard and smelled a demonstration of their need for purification. Then in the following chapters we read God's particular commands for maintaining cleanness. God gives laws about eating clean foods (Lev. 11), becoming clean after childbirth (Lev. 12), ensuring the people's cleanliness from diseases (Lev. 13–14), and promoting sexual cleanness (Lev. 15; 18). He details the requirements for the Sabbath and the feast days (Lev. 23), for property rights and care for the poor (Lev. 25), and for the proper fulfillment of vows (Lev. 27). Verse after verse, with exacting specificity, God tells his people how to be clean. While many of these laws occupy a unique place in covenant history and were fulfilled in Christ, we shouldn't miss the larger, enduring point: the holiness of God's people is extremely important to God.

We should notice two further things about these Old Testament laws. First, the call to cleanness arose from the covenant people's identity. "For I am the LORD who brought you up out of the land of Egypt to be your God. You shall therefore be holy, for I am holy," says the Lord (Lev. 11:45). God is perfectly holy, and Israel belonged to him: he separated them from the pagans and made a covenant with them, binding them to himself. They were the holy people of a holy God, and this changed everything about how they lived. Second, the call to cleanness was corporate. God declared each of these laws publicly and made them the responsibility of the whole covenant community. "Be holy, for I am holy," the Lord says again and again, not merely to individuals but to the gathered people of God (Lev. 11:44; see also 19:2; 20:7; 20:26; 21:8). Rooting out sexual sin and eradicating disease were tasks for the entire congregation.

It shouldn't surprise us then that holiness is also the corporate task of the church in this age. Peter quotes Leviticus when he writes to the churches, "As obedient children, do not be conformed to the passions of your former ignorance, but as he who called you is holy, you also be holy in all your conduct, since it is written, 'You shall be holy, for I am holy'" (1 Pet. 1:14–16). God separated us from our past worldliness and made us the holy people of a holy God. This means, then, that the church is a place (*the* place!) where holiness is valued. As we come together to the Lord's Table, and as we receive the water of baptism, God visibly distinguishes the members of our local church from the world and seals us as his own. In our neighborhoods and workplaces, we are surrounded by people who shrug indifferent shoulders at holiness or, worse, decry it as harmful to society. Our coworkers set their hope on the uncertainty of a paycheck. Our neighbors spend their weekends worshiping their lawn or their favorite quarterback. Our fellow students give their image-bearing bodies over to sinful desires and call it sexual empowerment. Every day, we live among idolaters and adulterers, among the greedy and the swindlers (cf. 1 Cor. 5:10). Only in the church is the call of God, "You shall be holy, for I am holy" (1 Pet. 1:16), taken seriously.

As it was for Israel, holiness is our community project. Those who belong to God's people have the God-given responsibility to promote holiness among all the saints. We also have the God-given privilege of being encouraged in holiness by our fellow saints. Let's consider five ways the local church is designed for our holiness.

1. Sanctification in Truth

First, in the church, we receive the sanctifying word. Jesus prayed for all of his disciples in every age, "Sanctify them in the truth; your word is truth" (John 17:17), and we saw earlier that "the apostles, the prophets, the evangelists, the shepherds and teachers" (Eph. 4:11) are Christ's gifts to equip the body of Christ to match Christ the head. Later in Ephesians, using a different analogy, Paul explains: "Christ loved the church and gave himself up for her, that he might sanctify her, *having cleansed her by the washing of water with the word*, so that he might present the church to himself in splendor, without spot or wrinkle or any such thing, that she might be holy and without blemish" (Eph. 5:25–27). When the word is read and preached in corporate worship, it is for our holiness. The word exposes our sin, holds up the righteousness of Christ, spurs us to repentance, and directs our conduct. It is "profitable for teaching, for reproof, for correction, and for training in righteousness" (2 Tim. 3:16). It washes us from our uncleanness. As the gathered saints submit to the word together, the Spirit makes us holy.

2. Help in Temptation

The church is also the place where we pray for one another's holiness. Our Lord taught us to pray, "Your will be done, on earth as it is in heaven" (Matt. 6:10), and, "Lead us not into temptation, but deliver us from evil" (Matt. 6:13), in part because holiness is a community project. The prayer he gave his disciples stands as a model for our own. As we pray together as the church—joining our hearts with the pastoral prayer and in church prayer meetings—and as we pray in private, we take up the cause of the church's holiness. Praying to *our* Father, we ask him to grant holiness to *us*. We pray that we would all be enabled to do God's will, and we pray that we would all be kept from temptation to sin. When Satan whispers poisonous enticements in your ear, remember that you do not stand alone. In that moment, the prayers of God's gathered people ascend before his throne and join the prayers of Christ himself, pleading for your perfect holiness. Satan halts, and sin relaxes its grip because God's people have prayed for you. The prayers of the whole church uphold the holiness of all the saints.

3. Models of Holiness

In the local church, too, we find examples of holy conduct among our fellow saints. Paul explains that "speaking the truth in love, we are to grow up in every way into him who is the head, into Christ, from whom the whole body, joined and held together by every joint with which it is equipped, when each part is working properly, makes the body grow so that it builds itself up in love" (Eph. 4:15–16). "Speaking the truth in love" is not merely a matter of saying the right words in the right way, though it is that. Paul's use of "speaking the truth" also has the broader meaning of "*holding* the truth" or "*adhering to* the truth."[6] One commentator even calls it "truthing."[7] In the church, we live according to the truth, and we live out the truth so that the whole body may grow into Christlikeness.

In the local church, we link arms with one another in our sanctification. One teenager resists sexual temptation at a school where seemingly no one else sees the point, but in his church his example encourages everyone who is likewise fleeing sexual immorality. One woman declines a job promotion because the new position would mean she could no longer care for her aging parents. She may be ridiculed in the office, but in the church she encourages all those—old and young—who are also seeking to honor mother and father, whatever it may cost them. One family with children devotes Sundays exclusively to worship, losing out on sports awards and athletic comraderie, but their example points the whole church to the "one thing necessary" (Luke 10:42). If we want to see Christlikeness, we have only to look as far as the people in the next pew. As Paul told the Corinthians, "Be imitators of me, as I am of Christ" (1 Cor. 11:1; cf. Phil. 3:17). We find in the local church a company of saints who are imitating Christ in all the circumstances of life. In the church, the saints live out the truth by grace, and the whole body is encouraged to holiness.

4. Promoting Holiness

Not only is the church the place where we see living examples of holiness; the church is also the place where we actively promote one another's holiness. Paul repeatedly urged the churches to consider the consciences of others when making choices about their own conduct (Rom. 14:1–23; 1 Cor. 8:1–13; 10:23–33). Our actions influence the saints around us, our holiness is connected to the holiness of the whole body, and we desire that every member would be kept from sin. As Christopher Ash explains:

> The individualistic and selfish insistence that I will do everything I am free in Christ to do, whether it be eating idol food (in Corinth) or eating bacon (in Rome), is not motivated by love. If I love someone and I understand just how important it is for them to maintain their integrity by doing only what their conscience allows, then I will do all I can to make it easy for them to do that.[8]

While our friends and neighbors give little thought to how their choices affect the convictions of others, our fellow saints love us enough to make seemingly personal choices with our holiness in mind. What the people of your local church choose to eat, drink, wear, listen to, watch, buy, or recommend is not just about them. It's also about you. In the church, we make it easy for others to be holy, whatever that may cost us. In the church, we set one another an example of holiness, and we live out the truth in a self-denying way in order to keep one another from stumbling.

5. Repentance and Restoration

Finally, we are built up in holiness by the restorative mission of the church. When we sin (and we do!), the church calls us to repentance. Our coworkers, neighbors, fellow students, and friends often have little concern for whether we sin—and sometimes they even lay the snares that entangle us. Only in the church do we find fellow saints who value our holiness enough to call us back when we wander. This happens in informal person-to-person exhortation, and it happens in the official disciplinary sanctions of the church. In the church, God has given us the privilege of restoration: "If anyone among you wanders from the truth and someone brings him back, let him know that whoever brings back a sinner from his wandering will save his soul from death and will cover a multitude of sins" (James 5:19–20). In the church, we have a community of people who are willing to lovingly warn us away from the soul-destroying brink of sin and who will lower a rescue rope if we ever tumble over.

A Holy End

With a final polish of the bathroom mirror, I step back to survey my work. Trash cans emptied? Check. Sink faucets gleaming? Check. Floors spotless? Check. Toilets scrubbed and paper towels replenished? Check and check. For one satisfying moment, the church is perfectly clean. Of course, it won't last forever. This evening, members will gather for a game night, and they are sure to leave pizza boxes and greasy fingerprints behind. The trash cans will again fill up, and, one speck at a time, new dust will accumulate. In this life, keeping the church clean is a never-ending task. It repeatedly points me to the day when the church's holiness will be complete.

Holiness is the church's beginning, and holiness is also our glorious end. As Charles Hodge writes, "The starting point and the goal of the church are identical. . . . We must be holy to belong to the church, and yet holiness is the ultimate perfection of the church."[9] We see this promised, final perfection in Ephesians 4:

> And [Christ] gave the apostles, the prophets, the evange-lists, the shepherds and teachers, to equip the saints for the work of ministry, for building up the body of Christ, until we all attain to the unity of the faith and of the knowledge of the Son of God, to mature manhood, to the measure of the stature of the fullness of Christ. (4:11–13)

The church's final, perfect, corporate holiness is Christ's ultimate goal. He desires all the saints to attain to unity, increase in
knowledge, become mature, and grow into his fullness (4:13).
As F. F. Bruce explains, "The glorified Christ provides the
standard at which his people are to aim: the corporate Christ
[the church] cannot be content to fall short of the personal
Christ."[10] The body must become a perfect match for Christ
the head. At times, we look at our frequent failings and those
of our fellow saints and wonder whether Christ's goals for
this body are not overly optimistic. But—thanks be to God!—
Christ is not the powerless head of a terminally ill body. Christ
is the triumphant mediator, the one in whom all the fullness of
God dwells (Col. 1:19). By his death and resurrection he unites
himself to his body, never to be separated from it. And with all
the fullness that dwells in him, he fills his church (Eph. 1:22–
23). Christ will make his whole body holy just as he is holy.

This is an encouragement to us in two ways. If, on the one
hand, we are prone to think too highly of ourselves and our
own spiritual progress, these verses remind us that our holiness
will not be complete until the holiness of every fingernail and
earlobe and eyelash of Christ's body has also been completed.[11]
Holiness is not a crowded ladder to personal advancement,
each person elbowing the others out of her way as she climbs.
Nor is holiness a solitary journey, each person setting out alone
on the road less traveled for the yet uncharted land of conformity to Christ. Nor is holiness a personal quest, each person
determining her own goals and leaving others to do the same.
Instead, in the church, my holiness is intimately connected to
the holiness of my fellow saints. If, on the other hand, we are
prone to despair over our own faltering holiness, these verses
remind us that our complete holiness is just as certain as the
holiness of the most eminent saints. Christ made us holy and
is making us holy—together. Christ fills us with his fullness—

together. Christ promises that we will all attain to perfect Christlikeness—together (Eph. 4:13). Martyn Lloyd-Jones writes, "The work is being done in every one of us; and every one of us has to be perfected; and as everyone is perfected, the whole will be perfected."[12]

Come, be holy.

7

Brothers and Sisters

MEMBERS OF THE FAMILY

Finally, brothers, rejoice. Aim for restoration, comfort
one another, agree with one another, live in peace;
and the God of love and peace will be with you.

2 CORINTHIANS 13:11

When I was a college student, I belonged to a church in the
middle of a Pennsylvania cornfield. Five hundred miles from
the church of my childhood, this was the first church I chose
for myself. In the early weeks of my college career, I had visited a variety of churches—walking into town from campus
or waiting on the sidewalk outside the dining hall for church
vans to pull up. Ultimately, though, I joined a small Presbyterian church twenty minutes from the school whose handful
of students relied on one another for rides. It was worth the
trip. Like the church where I grew up, this congregation took

the word of God seriously, worshiped sincerely, and loved one another deeply.

On the Sunday mornings we celebrated the Lord's Supper, the church service always ran so long that the main dining hall would be closed before our carload of students returned to campus. At this small-town college, the options for Sunday lunch were limited. With the cafeteria doors firmly locked, our next resort was a selection from the dorm vending machine. For students who attended both morning and evening worship, that package of stale peanut butter crackers might have to last until Monday's breakfast. The church could have ignored the situation, leaving us with crumbling Pop Tarts and rumbling bellies. They could have asked the pastor to shorten his sermon or skip the sacrament, leaving us with undernourished souls. They could have made insistent phone calls to the college or handed out brown-bag lunches at the church door. They could have. But, instead, they did something much better. They welcomed us home.

During four years as a college student and two years as a single professional, I ate countless meals in the homes of congregation members. I ate there on Sundays when the service ran late and on Sundays when it didn't. With other students, or by myself, I pulled up a folding chair to the tables of retired couples, families with children, and newlyweds. I had roast beef in the homes of farmers and lasagna in the homes of college faculty. I ate in one home so frequently that the family's weekly chicken-and-stuffing casserole became as familiar to me as my own mother's cooking. Between bites, the group around the table learned about one another's lives. And after lunch, more than one family assigned me to dish duty and then offered me a bed for an afternoon nap. In hindsight, these meals were not individually remarkable—they were ordinary lunches in ordinary houses with ordinary people—but over the span of weeks and years, they shaped my experience of belonging to that church. By feeding me lunch and then handing me a dish towel, these families welcomed me home. By opening their doors and then their hearts, they invited me to belong. I had no marital or biological ties to anyone in the congregation, and yet, in a very short time, they became my family.

Family of God

In this chapter we'll consider what it means for the members of the local church to be a family. The Greek word *adelphoi*—often translated as "brothers"—refers to "all the children of a family."[1] When Paul calls the gathered Corinthian church "brothers" (e.g., 1 Cor. 1:10), "my brothers" (e.g., 1 Cor. 1:11), "your own brothers" (1 Cor. 6:8), and "my beloved brothers" (1 Cor. 15:58), he affirms the close, familial relationship of every member of the church—whether male or female, Jew or Gentile, slave or free. Because we have Christ as our brother and God as our father, we have a sibling relationship with everyone who also belongs to the covenant family. This means that just as in a biological family,[2] the members of the church family have a common life together. We have mutual responsibilities toward one another, and as we care for one another, we experience—and display—the sibling love of Christ himself. In the local church, we are brothers and sisters. Welcome to the family.

Of all the descriptors in this book for the church, family is probably the easiest for us to observe in the Old Testament. One of the first things we learn when we read the Bible is that God's old-covenant people were a literal family. Adam and Eve received God's promise that their family would eventually yield a serpent-crushing savior. God rescued Noah and his family from the destruction of the world by hiding them in the ark. God entered into the covenant of circumcision with

Abraham and "[his] offspring after [him] throughout their generations" (Gen. 17:9). The priests served in the temple because they were sons and grandsons of Levi; the kings claimed their right to rule through the family line of David. Even the name of God's old-covenant people affirmed their familial relationship: they were called "Israel" because they were the descendants of Jacob, whom God named Israel (Gen. 32:28). In the Old Testament, we also have occasional glimpses of a family that extends beyond genetics—Rahab the pagan prostitute and Ruth the pagan widow both joined the genealogies of God's people—but generally God had a relationship with a people who had a familial relationship with each other.

Throughout the Old Testament, having a family indicates blessing. Spouses, children, and grandchildren are clear signs of God's favor, while the lack of family—being barren, orphaned, or widowed—is cause for deep lament. Many of God's gracious promises to his Old Testament people concern the future prosperity and growth of their family. God promised Abram (later, Abraham) a vast family:

> I will surely bless you, and I will surely multiply your offspring as the stars of heaven and as the sand that is on the seashore. And your offspring shall possess the gate of his enemies, and in your offspring shall all the nations of earth be blessed, because you have obeyed my voice. (Gen. 22:17–18; see also 15:5)

As a reward for Abraham's obedience, God promised him a family that would outnumber the stars and cover the earth like grains of sand. It's surprising, then, just how modest Abraham's family was. He was one hundred years old when his son Isaac was born and 160 when his twin grandsons, Esau and Jacob, were born. Fifteen years later, he died. In his lifetime, Abraham was the father of only a very small family. Even many generations later, the people who traced their lineage to Abraham were "the fewest of all peoples" (Deut. 7:7). But God's promises to Abraham—and to all whom he promised a family—did not fail. The book of Hebrews points us forward, telling us they "died in faith, not having received the things promised, but having seen them and greeted them from afar" (11:13).

When we come to the New Testament, we finally see a family tree with branches that stretch in all directions, to all the nations of the earth. As we have seen in previous chapters, the death and resurrection of Christ bring his beloved people into a relationship with him and with all others for whom he died. Jesus described this new relationship as a family:

> While [Jesus] was still speaking to the people, behold, his mother and his brothers stood outside, asking to speak to him. But he replied to the man who told him, "Who is my mother, and who are my brothers?" And stretching out his hand toward his disciples, he said, "Here are my mother and my brothers! For whoever does the will of my Father in heaven is my brother and sister and mother." (Matt. 12:46–50)

With this pronouncement, Jesus redefines his Israelite hearers' understanding of family in three ways. First, he places a high value on spiritual family, making it clear that his biological family is welcome to join them but can't expect to be preferred above them. His hearers expected him to prioritize his biological ties; Christ prioritizes his spiritual ones. Elsewhere, Christ even teaches that when a conflict arises between loyalty to biological family and loyalty to Christ and his family, the Christian must always align himself with Christ (e.g., Luke 14:26). Jesus next expands the perceived boundaries of this spiritual family, including everyone whose life—regardless of genetics—is marked by sincere godliness. Finally, he establishes his own centrality in the family, pointing his disciples to "the will of *my* Father" and naming them "*my* brother and sister and mother" (Matt. 12:50).[3] This passage makes clear that the people of God are not primarily or necessarily the descendants of Abraham or Isaac or Jacob. They are the family of Christ.

Our membership in this spiritual family is an essential part of our Christ-purchased identity and an important fulfillment of God's family promises to his old-covenant people. The story of the early church in the book of Acts reveals this truth. The first Christians gathered as local churches and did all things we expect families to do; they worshiped together, prayed together, ate together, and spent time together (Acts 2:42). They worked together toward the same goals (Act 4:31), and they shared their belongings to meet family members' needs (Acts 4:32–35). And God graciously blessed his New Testament family with extraordinary growth. He added to their numbers—by the thousands!—both individuals and biological families and both Jews and Gentiles. As the church in Jerusalem scattered over the face of the world to plant other churches and "make disciples of all nations" (Matt. 28:19), Christ's family became as numerous as the stars and as plentiful as sand on the seashore.

God never intended that his people be isolated individuals. When we belong to Christ, we belong to a vast family that stretches all the way back to Adam and Noah and Abraham and all the way forward to the heavenly "multitude that no one could number" (Rev. 7:9). But our place in this family is not abstract or theoretical. As Dietrich Bonhoeffer wrote, "Christian brotherhood is not an ideal which we must realize; it is rather a reality created by God in Christ in which we may participate."[4] We take our place in Christ's family by taking our place in the local church. Whether your congregation is small or large, urban or rural, generations-old or brand-new, it is no ordinary gathering. Every week, you worship alongside men, women, and children whom Christ calls his brothers and sisters and mothers. Together, you are the family of Jesus.

Life in the Household

I learned the significance of *brother* and *sister* long before I began to use those biblical terms myself. As a child, I would half listen to my parents' side of phone conversations, absorbed in a book but mildly curious about who was on the other end. The introductory chatter about an impending snowstorm or upcoming holiday could have been small talk with anyone from our neighbor to the garage mechanic. Even their transition to hushed pauses or solemn tones failed to fully engage my interest. But then I would hear my dad address the caller as "brother," and I would look up from the page. The person on the phone was undoubtedly a member of our church family, and whether he was calling about his ominous medical diagnosis or stopping by to borrow some chairs, it was probably going to impact my life.

If the local church is a family—and it is—then we can expect it to have very practical implications for our daily lives. Just as life in a biological family impacts everything from our schedule to our bank account, life in the spiritual family changes the way we live. In order to know what this family life is like, we can turn to the place where the Bible most frequently calls Christians "brothers and sisters": the New Testament Epistles. These letters to the churches are the family mission statement posted on the refrigerator. They are the family meeting agenda. They are the family rules. They are the family portrait. They tell us what it means to be brothers and sisters and teach us "how one ought to behave in the household of God" (1 Tim. 3:15). In these letters, we see that belonging to Christ's family reorients our allegiance, our affection, and our actions—not just on Sunday morning, but every hour of every day.

By their simple and repeated use of the term *brothers* (or *brothers and sisters*), the writers of the Epistles underscore that the people in the pews around us are, in fact, our family. Like the members of our biological family, we haven't chosen them for ourselves, but they have been chosen for us, and we are therefore inseparably bound to them. Because we are allied with Christ, we are allied with his family. In John's account of the crucifixion we read, "When Jesus saw his mother and the disciple whom he loved standing nearby, he said to his mother, 'Woman, behold your son!' Then he said to the disciple, 'Behold, your mother!' And from that hour the disciple took her to his own home" (John 19:26–27). At the declaration of Christ, Mary and John became family to one another and demonstrated all the loyalty we would expect from a biological mother and son. Similarly, the apostles reminded church members of their Christ-appointed family relationship, expecting that the fact of their spiritual kinship would transform their allegiance to one another. When Paul wanted the Roman church to welcome and help Phoebe, he called her "our sister" (Rom. 16:1); when Peter wanted to commend Silvanus, he called him "a faithful brother" (1 Pet. 5:12). Conversely, to illustrate the seriousness of Diotrephes's sinful rebellion, John reported that he "refuses to welcome the brothers, and also stops those who want to" (3 John 10). We ought to highly esteem the people who are, in fact, our family. If we don't, we are like a mother who willfully neglects her child or a child who selfishly abandons his aging parents.

What's more, our family loyalty ought to make disunity unthinkable. Paul addressed the Corinthian church as "brothers" and then warned them against petty divisions (1 Cor. 3:1–9); likewise, James called the members of the churches "my brothers" before condemning any hint of partiality (James 2:1). Peace and love ought to characterize the relationships of people who are brothers and sisters: "Finally, *brothers,*" writes Paul, "rejoice. Aim for restoration, comfort one another, agree with one another, live in peace; and the God of love and peace will be with you" (2 Cor. 13:11). These family terms are not incidental; they compel their hearers to live as the family they truly are. We, too, ought to think of—and speak of—our fellow church members as family. Committing to this family is not optional or incidental; it is a basic fact of our life in Christ. When we gather with the church, we should come with the declaration of Christ and the apostles ringing in our ears: Behold, your son! Behold, your mother! Behold, your brothers and sisters!

Having had our fundamental loyalties shaped by our unshakable family bond, we learn from the Epistles that we ought to cultivate sincere, heartfelt affection for the people in the local church. Acknowledging the fact of our sibling relationship is not an intellectual exercise; it's a profound truth that should stir deep emotions and overflow in tangible expression. Five times in the New Testament Epistles, God commands the members of the churches to demonstrate affection and love for one another, greeting one another with a "holy kiss" (Rom. 16:16; 1 Cor. 16:20; 2 Cor. 13:12; 1 Thess. 5:26; cf. 1 Pet. 5:14). Notably, these commands often come to us through the writing of the apostle Paul. Throughout Paul's ministry, he was often physically distant from the churches he loved. He could still pray for them, write to them, and send mutual friends to them, but what he really wanted was to be with them. Repeatedly, he expresses his desire to be present with the believers,[5] and repeatedly he commands them to be present with one another. From afar, Paul looks with longing at the gathered churches and tells them to be sure to get close to one another—close enough to touch. James, too, assumes that belonging to the local church will mean that we express affection for every brother and sister. The church member who tells the rich man to sit close and the poor man to stand far away has not understood life in God's family (James 2:2–4). In the church affection is not reserved for someone we especially like. It's also not withheld from someone we find awkward or difficult. We don't express affection only for the people of our choosing; we express affection for the people of God's covenant choosing. We "greet *all the brothers* with a holy kiss" (1 Thess. 5:26).

The people in the local church are our brothers and sisters—they are *Christ's* brothers and sisters—so we ought to regard them with all the delight and warmth of a healthy sibling relationship. We ought to cover their weaknesses with love and eagerly celebrate their advances in godliness (1 Pet. 4:8; 1 Thess. 3:6–10). We ought to cultivate in our hearts a determination to find and focus on whatever is pure and lovely and excellent and praiseworthy in them (Phil. 4:8). We ought to "love one another with brotherly affection" (Rom. 12:10). And in obedience to the Lord's command, we express our affection visibly and tangibly. We learn their names (3 John 15), and we find out their interests. When we see them in church on Sunday morning or in the grocery store on Thursday afternoon, we say hello. When there's an empty seat next to them at the church dinner or on the commuter train, we sit there. When we pass in the hallway or on the sidewalk, we greet them with "a holy kiss." And in a context where a literal kiss would be out of place, we still fulfill this command with a culturally appropriate, morally chaste, physical expression of love. We extend a hand on a shoulder, a warm smile with a hand clasp, or a friendly hug. We reach out again and again with a closeness that publicly affirms our family bond. And by these things we say without reservation and without partiality, "You are my brothers and sisters, and I love you."[6]

Acknowledging the truth of our family relationship and cultivating affection within our family bond then encourages us to willingly take up our family responsibilities. Throughout the New Testament, God commands us to mutual care in the local church. These "one another" commands are instructions for our family life. Belonging to the church will always increase our obligations and decrease our independence. And this is good. As brothers and sisters in the Lord, we should encourage one another's spiritual maturity: build up one another (1 Thess. 5:11), admonish one another (Col. 3:16), lovingly speak truth to one another (Eph. 4:15), speak to one another in song (Eph. 5:19), exhort one another (Heb. 3:13), stir up one another to love and good works (Heb. 10:24), and pray for one another (James 5:16). As members of the same family, we should meet one another's temporal needs: care for one another (1 Cor. 12:25), serve one another (Gal. 5:13), bear one another's burdens (Gal. 6:2), comfort one another (2 Cor. 13:11), and show hospitality to one another (1 Pet. 4:9). As those whom Christ brought into his family by his own blood, we should respond to one another with love: forgive one another (Col. 3:13), be patient with one another (Eph. 4:2), submit to one another (Eph. 5:21), and confess sin to one another (James 5:16). And, as those who belong to one another, our brothers' and sisters' joys and sorrows should actually become our own: "Rejoice with those who rejoice," writes Paul, "weep with those who weep" (Rom. 12:15).

These commands—and the many more like them throughout the Epistles—remind us that life in Christ's family has specific, concrete implications for every day of our lives. Of course, caring for family is sometimes frustrating and often tiring—ask any mother of toddlers or adult child of elderly parents—and loving the local church is no different. Our brothers and sisters in Christ are not always agreeable or thankful, and meeting their needs requires great sacrifice, but it is precisely because they are our brothers and sisters that we do. The church is not a man-made society that we can participate in—or opt out of—according to our own level of comfort. The PTA, the neighborhood association, or the library booster club do not obligate us to personal sacrifice when things get tough. Family does. Because God's people are our family, we will hold our own preferences and priorities loosely (Acts 4:32; Phil. 2:3–4). We will open our hearts and our doors; we will pull up another chair to the dinner table and add another name to our prayer list. We will give them our groceries and furniture and smiles. We will share their grief and trials and disappointments. We will look for ways to show love. As a result, we will expect to have less money and less free time than we would have on our own. We will expect to have added sorrow. We will also expect to have great joy.

Jesus, Our Brother

Ultimately, our joy in our spiritual family comes from something greater than our daily experience of life with the ordinary people who belong to the local church. Our joy comes from Christ, our brother, who is making everyone in the family like himself. Romans 8 tells us that "those whom he foreknew he also predestined to be conformed to the image of his Son, in order that he might be the firstborn among many brothers" (8:29). The whole work of redemption has this in view: a vast family where all the members look increasingly like their older brother. Knowing this, we can delight in the particular people God has given us as brothers and sisters, no matter how unexceptional they may seem, because in them we apprehend something of Christ. As they grow and mature in the family circle, their character and conduct become more and more like the one our souls love best. Because of the work of his Spirit, they speak his words, love his ways, hate his enemies, reflect his holiness, and serve his ends. We want to be with them, and we want to care for them because we want to see Christ displayed in them. And the more they—and we—become like Christ, the more we will love them.[7]

In one of Scripture's most striking statements, we read that Christ looks at the people of his church and "is not ashamed to call them brothers" (Heb. 2:11). How can this be? How can Christ look at the ordinary, weak, and sometimes difficult people of his family and not be ashamed? He is not ashamed because he is increasingly being formed in them, and he is confident that one day—because of his work on their behalf— their transformation will be complete (Heb. 2:10–18; see also Gal. 4:19). He willingly identifies with us because our identity is found in him. As we affirm our relationship to the people of our local church and overflow with affection for them, we testify loudly to the world that we are not ashamed to call them brothers either—not because they are perfect but because they are being made like our only sibling who is. In our Christian brothers and sisters we can see something the world cannot. We can see Christ himself.

Come, belong to the family.

8

Gospel Partners

WE HAVE WORK TO DO

I thank my God in all my remembrance of
you . . . because of your partnership in the gospel
from the first day until now.

PHILIPPIANS 1:3, 5

Summer darkness settles around the church building—the bats
swoop around its eaves, and the frogs begin their guttural chorus. Inside, most of the rooms are dark too. But down the back
hallway a light is on. In one room, seated on chairs arranged
in a circle, the church gathers. A handful of people—a few
of them elderly, a few children, a few singles, a few married
couples—bow their heads and close their eyes. One by one
we take turns leading the others in prayer. We pray for perse-
cuted congregations on the other side of the world; we pray
for fledgling churches on the other side of the state; we pray
for the success of the gospel in our own community. We bring

before the Lord names of specific people who do not yet know him. We ask the Lord to send out workers into his harvest field. We plead for boldness for workers who are already laboring. With one accord, we petition the Father to build his church and glorify his name. We ask him to send his Spirit. And then, in the name of the Son and with a chorus of amens, we are finished. We raise our heads and open our eyes, exchanging a few words with the people around us. We gather our belongings, and we walk out into the night.

Humanly speaking, a church prayer meeting doesn't look like much. A group of people spending an hour with their eyes closed taking turns addressing an unseen God is unlikely to draw the acclaim of the world. At best, it seems like a quaint ritual. At worst, outright foolishness. Our unbelieving friends and neighbors place little value on an uncomfortable, time-consuming, spiritual practice that has no tangible or immediate results. The people of the world dismiss our intercessions with barely a thought. But though they don't know it, the church at prayer is their very best friend. People walking in darkness have no better ally than a group of believers on their knees, united in the work of pleading for the light of Christ to shine in their undying souls.

So far in this book, we have seen many glorious truths about the church. We have heard God's resounding declaration that—no matter how unimpressive or weak or struggling—the local church is beloved by him, called to be his people, gathered to worship, given shepherds, granted gifts, made holy, and joined as a family. In the church, we experience all the fullness of Christ. Now we will widen our gaze and consider our work in the world. "Go therefore," Christ charged his church, "and make disciples of all nations, baptizing them in the name of the Father and of the Son and of the Holy Spirit, teaching them to observe all that I have commanded you" (Matt. 28:19–20).

As this chapter unfolds, we'll see that the church's disciple-making mission is an all-hands-on-deck congregational task with each member contributing to the work.[1] The church powerfully proclaims to the world the good news of Christ, and its members are coworkers. Writing to the church at Philippi, Paul reflected on the missionary work that had taken him throughout the known world, and he testified to the valuable labor of those who stayed behind: "I thank my God . . . because of your partnership in the gospel from the first day until now" (Phil. 1:3, 5). Like the Philippians, God's people today participate together in the advance of the gospel. When the local church engages in the work of living for God's glory, of praying persistently, and of giving generously, we become partners in the gospel and, ultimately, partakers together of grace. It may not look like much, but it's one of the most important jobs in the world.

Fellow Workers

In the last chapter we considered God's promise to give Abraham a vast family that would cover the earth: "I will surely bless you, and I will surely multiply your offspring as the stars of heaven and as the sand that is on the seashore. And your offspring shall possess the gate of his enemies, and in your offspring shall all the nations of earth be blessed, because you have obeyed my voice" (Gen. 22:17–18). That same promise also gives us a starting point for understanding God's work in the world and his people's part in it.[2] From the earliest chapters of the Bible, we see that "all the nations of the earth" have a place in God's redemptive plan and that God will use his people to bless all peoples.

Although the Old Testament doesn't reveal exactly *how* this will happen, it is unequivocal in declaring that it *will* happen.[3] In one passage after another, we read joyful descriptions of

115

what it will look like when the nations are blessed and come to know the Lord as their God. The psalms, in particular, overflow with missionary expectation. They delight in the day when stories of the Lord's blessing on Israel will be a compelling invitation to worldwide praise:

> Declare his glory among the nations,
>   his marvelous works among all peoples! . . .
>
> Ascribe to the LORD, O families of the peoples,
>   ascribe to the LORD glory and strength! . . .
>   bring an offering and come into his courts!" (Ps.
>   96:3, 7–8)

They wait for the day when "all the earth" will obediently "serve the LORD with gladness" (Ps. 100:1–2). They look for the day when all peoples will bring worship to God alone: "All the nations you have made shall come and worship before you, O LORD, and shall glorify your name" (Ps. 86:9). The Old Testament repeatedly anticipates a time when "all the families of the nations" (Ps. 22:27) will together serve and worship the Lord.

These psalms, what one writer calls "the music of missions,"[4] would have been regularly on the lips—and in the hearts—of the Israelites. It's fitting then, that stirred by the vision of what would be, God's people joined together to ask him to bring it to pass:

> On your walls, O Jerusalem,
>   I have set watchmen;
> all the day and all the night
>   they shall never be silent.
>
> You who put the Lord in remembrance,
>   take no rest,
> and give him no rest

until he establishes Jerusalem
and makes it a praise in the earth. (Isa. 62:6–7)

Jerusalem was the place of God's presence and the center of true worship. By asking God to make it a praise in the earth (Isa. 62:7), the Israelites expressed their longing to see people from all nations bowing before the Lord in worship. And they didn't just pray for this casually or occasionally; they prayed for it "all the day and all the night" (62:6). The people who knew the Lord wanted others to know him too. They prayed for it in the congregation and in their homes, when they got up and when they went to bed, from their earliest childhood lispings to their deathbed exhalations. On their knees, God's people took no rest, and they gave God no rest. In light of his glorious promises, they asked him to act.

And he did. Christ came into the world, lived a life of perfect obedience, died for the sins of his people, rose from the tomb, and ascended into heaven. On the cross, he was lifted up so all the earth might worship. Then in his last earthly instructions to his gathered disciples, he gave them the marching orders they had been anticipating for thousands of years: "All authority in heaven and on earth has been given to me. Go therefore and make disciples of all nations, baptizing them in the name of the Father and of the Son and of the Holy Spirit, teaching them to observe all that I have commanded you" (Matt. 28:18–20). On the mountain, the head of the church declared the mission of the church to the members of the church: Go and make disciples.

It's not uncommon to hear it said that the Old Testament presents an invitation for the nations to *come in*, and the New Testament gives an imperative for God's people to *go out*. This has an element of truth: *going out* to proclaim good news is the unique focus of the New Testament age, and *coming in* to the place of God's worship is the repeated vision of the Old

Testament. But we shouldn't dismiss the fact that the New Testament emphasizes both *going out* and *coming in*. The early church went *out* ("go" 28:19), but their goal was to bring people *in* to the knowledge of God in Christ, to the sacraments, and to the fellowship of his church ("make disciples . . . baptizing them . . . [and] teaching them," 28:19–20).[5] The Old Testament prophesied a time when people from all nations would gather to worship God and learn to obey him. The Christ-given mission of the New Testament church fulfills it.

Detailing the period following Jesus's ascension, Acts and the Epistles show us in greater detail how the church undertakes its commission. In Acts we see that disciple making and church planting are intrinsically connected. Wherever the apostles went, they preached the gospel and established local churches among those who believed. Beginning in Jerusalem and throughout Asia and even to Rome itself, the gospel advanced by the preaching of God's appointed messengers. The churches at Ephesus, Philippi, Galatia, Colossae, and Corinth—congregations familiar to any reader of the New Testament—began through the missionary efforts of gospel preachers. And those churches, in turn, invested in the planting of gospel seed in their communities and in faraway places. Lest we believe first-century gospel success was the single-handed work of a few men, the Epistles reaffirm that the mission of the church belonged to the entire church. Repeatedly, Paul thanks the churches for their gifts, asks the churches for their prayers, and commends the churches for their faithful gospel witness. Though the preachers may have been out front, they never worked alone; the gathered people of God were their indispensable partners.

We see this whole-church partnership clearly in the greetings that Paul offered in many of his letters. By mentioning specific church members, Paul testified to the connection he felt with other believers who participated in disciple making in their own cities and throughout the world. Again and again he named them as coworkers in the missionary task. As we might expect, he publicly aligned with men who, like himself, labored in teaching and preaching the word, calling Timothy and Titus, for example, his fellow workers (Rom. 16:21; 2 Cor. 8:23). But some of Paul's "fellow workers" were much more surprising. He used this term for Prisca and Aquila, the married couple who quietly discipled Apollos (Acts 18:24–26; Rom. 16:3). He used it for the family of Stephanas, who served the other members of the Corinthian church from its beginning (1 Cor. 16:15–16). He even used it for Euodia and Syntyche, the two quarreling women from the Philippian church (Phil. 4:3). The great apostle Paul affirmed his partnership in the gospel work with elders and nonelders, with men and women, with parents and children, and with church members whose conduct could be embarrassingly immature. When Paul thought of the local churches throughout the world, he thought of them as vital to the spread of the gospel. They may have seemed insignificant, but he knew the truth. They were his fellow workers.

Entering into Gospel Partnership

My church recently took a collection to fund the first translation of three books of the Bible into the language spoken by the Angave people in the Papua New Guinea jungle. The husband and wife who worked on the translation have lived in an Angave village for decades. There are no roads to the place where they live. No electric grid. No grocery stores. But there are a few thousand people who have never heard the good news of Christ crucified for sinners, so day after day the husband preaches the Bible, and the wife teaches the people to read. Together they work to translate Scripture. When they needed money to travel to another part of the jungle to have their

119

translations checked for accuracy, my church committed to pay their expenses. The money we sent to Papua New Guinea—just over two thousand dollars in two months' time—was not a huge amount in absolute terms, but it required sacrifice from the members of our small church. One Sunday I watched my own children remove money from their mason jars of savings: a sum that had taken them years to accumulate and only a few minutes to decide to give. They placed it in the offering plate and followed it with their eyes as it traveled across the congregation. Suddenly they were three boys with empty piggy banks. They were also partners in the gospel.

Throughout his letter to the church at Philippi, Paul highlights three aspects of the Philippians' partnership with him. By living lives worthy of the gospel, praying at all times, and giving generously, the local church worked alongside Paul for the cause of Christ in the world.[6] These marks of Philippian gospel partnership should mark our congregations too. We ought to display, in the words of one commentator, a "hearty co-operation in the work of the gospel."[7] Let's consider how—practically—the local church enters into gospel partnership in these three areas.

Although it might seem counterintuitive, one of the most important ways the local church can support gospel work throughout the world is by maintaining a faithful witness in the place where its members live and worship. Paul writes, "Only let your manner of life be worthy of the gospel of Christ, so that whether I come and see you or am absent, I may hear of you that you are standing firm in one spirit, with one mind striving side by side for the faith of the gospel, and not frightened in anything by your opponents" (Phil. 1:27–28). Behavior that is "worthy of the gospel" is not, of course, behavior that *merits* God's grace in the gospel. Instead, it is behavior *shaped by* the gospel and behavior that therefore *promotes* the gospel.[8] When people who belong to Christ act like people who belong to Christ, they will exalt Christ in the world. All of the truths we have seen so far in this book are part of the church's gospel labor; when we love one another, worship God according to his word, submit to Christ's appointed authority, and grow in holiness together, we display before the world the transforming power of the Spirit and testify to the loveliness of Christ.

Behavior worthy of the gospel has two gospel-magnifying effects. First, it serves as a testimony to the lost and dying in our own community. By living consistent gospel lives, we encourage our unbelieving friends and neighbors to embrace the good news of Christ for themselves. By speaking a word of Christ to those we know, we invite others to be his disciples. Even when we encounter people who remain opposed to the gospel ("your opponents," 1:28), our godly behavior allows us to face their accusations with a clear conscience and confidence in our salvation. Second, when we act like gospel people, we encourage other gospel people. When the Philippians lived Christlike lives, they stood with one another and with Paul in the work of the gospel ("striving side by side for the faith of the gospel," 1:27). And when ungodly people responded with hostility, the Philippians had an opportunity to share in Paul's struggles. Their battle with worldly unbelief was "the same conflict" (1:30) Paul battled where he was. If we in the local church commit ourselves to biblical worship, godly language, a right use of time, respect for those in authority, sexual purity, love for our neighbors, and bold evangelism, we will welcome people to Christ. We will also face opposition and ridicule. But in all things—and without even leaving town—we will stand side by side with our fellow workers throughout the world, refreshing their hearts as they strive for the same countercultural, Christ-exalting, gospel-shaped life.

The next way the Philippian church entered into gospel partnership was prayer. Paul prayed faithfully for the Philippians (Phil. 1:3–4), and he knew the church was praying for him (Phil. 1:19). He was confident that their prayers would be an instrument for the spread of the gospel: "I know that through your prayers and the help of the Spirit of Jesus Christ this will turn out for my deliverance" (Phil. 1:19). Throughout the Epistles Paul asked the various churches to pray. He asked them to pray for him to preach with clarity and boldness (Eph. 6:19–20; Col. 4:4), to have open doors to proclaim Christ (Col. 4:3–4), and to be rescued from the wicked designs of ungodly people (Rom. 15:31; 2 Thess. 3:2). He asked them to pray "that the word of the Lord may speed ahead and be honored, as happened among you" (2 Thess. 3:1). Paul knew that the disciple-making task of the church is a spiritual mission, and only the Spirit can open blind eyes, unstop deaf ears, clear sin-clouded minds, and quicken dead hearts. Only the Spirit can draw men and women to Christ and make men and women like Christ, so—by prayer—we must ask him to work. Like God's people in Isaiah's day, we take no rest and give God no rest as we pray together for the success of the gospel (Isa. 62:6–7). The prayers of God's people are not supplemental to gospel ministry; they are essential.

When the local church prays for those who preach the gospel, we labor alongside them. As Paul exhorted the church at Rome, "I appeal to you . . . to strive together with me in your prayers" (Rom. 15:30). And when he wrote to the Colossian church, he commended a man who had labored hard for the good of their souls: "Epaphras, who is one of you, a servant of Christ Jesus, greets you, always struggling on your behalf in his prayers, that you may stand mature and fully assured in all the will of God. For I bear him witness that he has worked hard for you and for those in Laodicea and in Hierapolis"

(Col. 4:12–13). Paul's commendation highlights a surprising location for Epaphras's hard work on behalf of the churches: a prayer meeting. Although a congregation of Christians with heads bowed and eyes closed—asking the Lord to bless his word in the local church and on the other side of the world—doesn't look like it's accomplishing much, Scripture assures us it is. In response to the prayers of his people, God sends laborers into his harvest field (Luke 10:2), extinguishes Satan's flaming darts (Eph. 6:16–20; cf. Ps. 8:2), revives saints (2 Chron. 7:13–14), saves sinners (2 Chron. 7:13–14; James 5:14–15), and pours just judgment on the earth (Rev. 8:3, 5). As the local church, we must not be tempted to eliminate or abbreviate corporate prayer; praying together for the advance of Christ's kingdom should be a priority for our church life (cf. Matt. 6:10; Acts 2:42). In worship services and at prayer meetings, we strive together with far-flung gospel laborers. The church on its knees is the church hard at work.[9]

A third aspect of gospel partnership is giving. Paul wrote that "no church entered into partnership with me in giving and receiving, except you only" (Phil. 4:15), applying his earlier "partnership" language to the Philippians' financial generosity. Our monetary giving is a partnership in the most concrete terms. When we support the work of the church in our own congregation and in other places, we participate in gospel proclamation. This is a responsibility for every member of Christ's church. Our money turns on the lights, opens the doors, feeds and clothes and sends gospel preachers, purchases Bibles, makes copies and coffee, and assists people in need. We all know that those who preach sow gospel seed (Ps. 126:6; 1 Cor. 3:6–8), but so do those who give. Our homes, cars, portfolios, and paychecks are more than they first appear. Paul says our financial resources are God-given "seed for sowing" (2 Cor. 9:10). When we give generously, we sow seed in kingdom soil and can expect a "harvest of . . . righteousness" in our own hearts and in the hearts of others (2 Cor. 9:10).

When we give, we also partner with gospel workers in self-denial. Paul himself had sacrificed much for the sake of Christ (Phil. 4:10–13), and when the Philippians sacrificed from their own resources, they shared his trouble (Phil. 4:14). By your gifts—denying yourself treats and comfort and even basic necessities—you come alongside men and women who do the same every single day so that Christ might be proclaimed in the world. And this precious partnership of sacrificial giving belongs to both rich and poor. Paul commends the Macedonian churches this way: "In a severe test of affliction, their abundance of joy and their extreme poverty have overflowed in a wealth of generosity on their part. For they gave according to their means, as I can testify, and beyond their means, of their own accord, begging us earnestly for the favor of taking part in the relief of the saints" (2 Cor. 8:2–4). The Macedonians faced "extreme poverty," but they still gave because partnership in the gospel ("the favor of taking part," 8:4) motivated them. The privilege of being fellow workers ought to motivate us too. Whether we sow the word or sow our money, whether we give up comfort or give up our paycheck, whether we plant churches on the other side of the world or contribute from our hometown, God's people are partners in the gospel.

Partakers of Grace

Just as surely as the ordinary people of the local church participate in the hard work of gospel ministry, we will also participate in the joy of the gospel's reward. Paul says to the Philippian church: "You are all partakers with me of grace, both in my imprisonment and in the defense and confirmation of the gospel" (Phil. 1:7). The church partnered with Paul in his struggles, so they shared in the same abundant grace. In the words of Matthew Henry: "Those who suffer with the saints are and shall be comforted with them; and those shall share in the reward, who bear their part of the burden."[10] At the end of a hard day of gospel work, we can await the Spirit's refreshment and encouragement. When our bank account dwindles and our free time disappears, we can look for the Lord to supply our needs and multiply his glory. During long years of persistent prayer, we can anticipate a harvest of souls. Our Lord delights to show kindness to his faithful servants. As the local church pursues Christ, prays fervently, and gives generously, we can expect the Lord's help for every day and his "well done" on the last one. In that day, he will welcome all his workers into the eternal kingdom "'that they may rest from their labors, for their deeds follow them!'" (Rev. 14:13).

In eternity, when we are finally gathered with our Angave brothers and sisters who studied the Bible with Spirit-opened eyes and trusted in Christ with Spirit-enabled faith, the members of my church will have a share in the heavenly rejoicing. We will worship in the near presence of Christ, hand in hand with everyone who gave and prayed and worked for the spread of the gospel in Papua New Guinea. The children who emptied their piggy banks and the elderly women who prayed in their homes will stand together with the Bible translators, and the Lamb will receive all the glory. The members of the local church may seem insignificant, but from the perspective of heaven, they are vital partners in the work of the gospel.

Come, we have work to do.

9

Multitude

PART OF SOMETHING BIGGER

After this I looked, and behold, a great multitude
that no one could number, from every nation, from
all tribes and peoples and languages, standing
before the throne and before the Lamb.

REVELATION 7:9

Several times each year, our church has its Sunday evening worship service with other gospel-preaching churches in the area. Last Sunday was one of those. As I made my way down the hall toward the sanctuary, the approaching worshipers— both Baptists and Presbyterians—greeted one another by name with cries of delight and warm hugs. They asked about one another's work and family; they learned news from one another's churches. Glancing out the window, I could see the same thing happening in the parking lot. Some people made it only a few steps past their cars before recognizing other beloved saints they hadn't seen in months. Progress toward the church doors was slow, and passersby must have wondered at the obvious affection among characteristically stoic New Englanders.

Once inside, we found seats. Four congregations in one room forced each of us to move over, sit close, and make room. The voices of four congregations swelled the familiar hymns of praise, and the amens of four congregations encouraged each pastor who led us in prayer. With one accord, we confessed the faith of Christians in all ages and places; with one heart, we received the preached word of our God. Dismissed under the same benediction, we shared cookies and more stories in the fellowship hall. And outside, the children ran together across the evening spring grass, making new friends over tag and hide-and-seek until the moment it was time to go.

Meeting in a place that a recent study called "the most post-Christian city in America,"[1] our combined assembly is never large, but it is always immensely encouraging. Week by week, vastly outnumbered by our avowedly secular neighbors, our individual churches can sometimes seem like minor oddities. But every few months for two hours on a Sunday evening, these scattered congregations gather. We sing together, pray together, confess our faith together, receive the word together, and fellowship together. Together, we affirm that though each local church may appear weak and solitary, we have never been—and will never be!—alone.

In this final chapter, we'll have an opportunity to delight in what one confession calls "the communion of churches."[2] Having explored our fellowship and mutual responsibilities within the local church, we'll now see how congregations relate to one another. According to Scripture, this has always been the practice of God's people, and it will be our glorious practice for all eternity. In the local church, we are not just a few or a few hundred; we are part of something much, much bigger. We are part of the multitude.

Bound Firmly Together

Although connections between local churches become established only after Christ's ascension, we certainly see seeds of interchurch relations in the Old Testament. Long before the book of Acts, the Bible reveals a pattern of smaller assemblies that have communion with one another while belonging to a larger assembly. The people of God were organized as tribes: twelve unique families with a corporate identity as a single nation. And, while God strictly forbade intimacy with the surrounding pagans, he allowed the members of each tribe to marry, worship, and work with members from other tribes because, together, they were his people. This common identity as a corporate people also obligated them to care for one another. When Israel entered the Promised Land, the tribes of Reuben and Gad sought permission to settle on the east side of the Jordan River. Although they weren't making their homes in the same location as the others, the Lord required these tribes to assist the rest of the tribes to subdue the land (Num. 32). As part of Israel, the tribes had a duty to help one another eradicate wickedness, secure peace, and establish a place of worship. Later, sadly, the tribes often failed to fulfill their mutual obligations. When the tribe of Benjamin refused to participate in the investigation of a crime and then did not listen to counsel from their fellow Israelites, the other tribes understood their inaction as deliberate rebellion (Judg. 20). And when Deborah's army defeated pagan King Sisera, her victory song chided the tribes who did not stand with the rest of God's people in battle: "Why did you sit still among the sheepfolds, to hear the whistling for the flocks?" (Judg. 5:16). Throughout the Old Testament, it was the duty of groups of

God's people to have robust relationships with other groups of God's people. When they stood aloof, it was nothing less than a sign of apostasy.

In the kingdom of Israel, the highest expression of intertribal communion took place at the temple at Jerusalem.[3] Psalm 122, one of the songs Israelites would sing together as they went up to the temple, delights in the regular gathering of the tribes:

> Jerusalem—built as a city
>> that is bound firmly together,
> to which the tribes go up,
>> the tribes of the LORD,
> as was decreed for Israel. (122:3–4)

The worshipers going to the temple rejoiced at the thought that they'd be joined there by other groups of God's people from other places and that the whole company would be united before the Lord. Jerusalem was the place where Israelites joined their voices and hearts in praise ("to give thanks to the name of the LORD," 122:4). With all the worshiping tribes gathered within her walls, Jerusalem was indeed "bound firmly together" (122:3). Compelled by this reality, the Israelites weren't content to merely *imagine* the unity of God's people; they wanted to actually *experience* it. They wanted to set the soles of their feet on the same courtyard as the members of all the tribes, and they were willing to take thousands of dusty steps to get there. At the end of a long journey, "Our feet have been standing within your gates, O Jerusalem!" is the joyful shout of finally joining the glorious multitude (122:2).

When we come to the New Testament age, tribal distinctions fade under our new identity in Christ (Gal. 3:28), and our locus of worship is no longer a city but is Christ himself (Heb. 12:22–24). Nevertheless, the old-covenant pattern of robust communion between congregations continues to be essential. The coming of Christ does not diminish "the peace of Jerusalem" (Ps. 122:6); rather, Christ brings his people into greater unity, greater cooperation, and greater opportunities for worship together. Christ is the one head of his church in all places and at all times (Eph. 1:22; 5:23; Col. 1:18), and his atoning work "unite[s] all things in him, things in heaven and things on earth" (Eph. 1:10). This includes our various congregations. Wherever they meet, Christ's people are our people, the gospel they proclaim is the gospel we proclaim, and we must bow together before Christ our king. Interestingly, when Luke reports on the earliest spread of the gospel, he describes it as the growth of a single church: "So the church throughout all Judea and Galilee and Samaria had peace and was being built up. And walking in the fear of the Lord and in the comfort of the Holy Spirit, it multiplied" (Acts 9:31). Congregations assembled for worship in various locations in Judea and Galilee and Samaria. They were unique groups of specific people under the care of particular elders. But seen together through the lens of Christ's great redeeming work, they were "the church."[4]

Many of the things that we have already noted in this book about the reality of unity and diversity among members of churches are also true about the churches themselves. When Jesus prayed that his followers would be "one even as we are one" (John 17:22), he looked for the Father to grant accord within churches but also between churches. When Paul wrote about "one body" and "many members," he was talking about our unity in the local church and also about unity among churches (1 Cor. 12:12). When he reminded church members of the "one hope" and "one faith" they shared, he was speaking both locally and globally (Eph. 4:4–6).[5] The people of God throughout the world are, in fact, unified. Your own local church and the gospel-proclaiming church in the next town—or across the street—have a real, spiritual connection. We have various gifts but one Spirit; various opportunities for service but one Lord; various kingdom activities but the same empowering God (cf. 1 Cor. 12:4–6). It's fitting, then, that we would express our invisible union in practical, tangible, visible ways. Like the tribes who left their comfortable homes to fight on behalf of the other tribes, and like the groups of Israelites who journeyed from afar to worship with the whole assembly in Jerusalem, churches ought to express robust relationships with one another.

Communion of Churches

Before we look at the specific ways our local churches express and nurture their unity, we should recognize that there are a variety of convictions about church polity represented in the church of Christ. But even for those of us who believe the communion of churches should be formal and binding,[6] simply acknowledging the importance of official relationships should never become a substitute for the vigorous, lived-out cooperation that such polity is meant to promote. The Bible repeatedly gives specific examples of how New Testament churches wholeheartedly loved and cared for one another. In this section we will discuss five biblical aspects of interchurch communion, and it is my hope that all readers will delight in and seek to apply them.[7]

Our local churches are one in Christ. Let's make our unity tangible.

1. Information

At some of our joint worship services, we take a few minutes for the pastor of each church to give a report from that church. Recently, we heard about a husband and wife from one church who were heading to Madagascar to serve the cause of Christ there. We heard about a series of evangelistic seminars in another church and a series of new babies in a third. We heard reports about elder and deacon candidates, about recent converts, and about the deaths of faithful saints. To an outsider, these snippets of information wouldn't seem particularly newsworthy. To the members of the gathered churches, they were precious testimonies to God's work in our midst.

Passing information from one church to another—whether as an official report or a grocery-store-aisle exchange between members—is a vital practice. By it, our churches affirm their commitment to one another's spiritual health and receive kingdom news that spurs all of our other interchurch practices. Paul frequently passed information from one church to another, sending his reports by the hand of a trusted messenger (e.g., Eph. 6:21–22; Col. 4:7–9). This wasn't a mere formality; his letter to the Thessalonian church demonstrates the spirit in which we should seek and receive such information: "When I could bear it no longer, I sent to learn about your faith" (1 Thess. 3:5). Paul wasn't dozing through the church reports; he was desperate for them. Then, having heard good news about the Thessalonians' progress in faith, Paul overflowed in love (3:6), received comfort (3:7), thanked God (3:9), expressed joy (3:9), and prayed for them "night and day" (3:10). We, too, should take great interest in the faith of churches near and far. We should ask members how their congregations are doing; we should encourage our elders as they meet with elders from other churches; we should receive email reports from churches around the world with a sense of urgent expectation. We should rejoice and give thanks to God when we hear good news about other churches. This is not just any news. This is news of Christ's work in the world and among his beloved people. It heartens us, strengthens us, and moves us to pray. It is news of the greatest significance.

2. Prayer

In our joint services, we immediately follow the church reports with a time of prayer for those churches. The information we know about other churches ought to prompt our supplications on their behalf. "From the day we heard," wrote Paul to the Colossian church, "we have not ceased to pray for you" (1 Thess. 1:9). Elsewhere, Paul urged the Ephesian church to persevere in prayer for "all the saints" (Eph. 6:18). All of the things we pray for our own congregation, we ought to pray for the churches with whom we have communion. During Sunday worship services or in a midweek prayer meeting, we can pray for their gospel proclamation (2 Thess. 3:1), spiritual maturity (Col. 1:9–14), and ministry and missions (Matt. 9:37–38). We also ought to pray for churches in crisis. The writer to the Hebrews urges: "Remember those who are in prison, as though in prison with them, and those who are mistreated, since you also are in the body" (Heb. 13:3). When we hear that other churches are facing persecution, mistreatment, or attacks from the evil one, we ought to pray for them as a congregation—not just occasionally or casually but "as though in prison with them." This prayerful communion among churches is rooted in our real, spiritual communion; we pray for them "since [we] also are in the body." On our knees as a church, we lift up other churches. We "rejoice with those who rejoice," "weep with those who weep," and "bear one another's burdens" (Rom. 12:15; Gal. 6:2). In prayer, our churches come together before the throne of God.

3. Contribution

Our spiritual concern for one another overflows into practical assistance. In the last chapter we discussed the importance of financial generosity toward Christ's work in the world. This isn't merely an obligation to support frontline missionaries in unreached parts of the earth; it's also an obligation to help other local churches in need, whether near or far. Paul urged the Corinthian church to make a "willing gift" for the relief of the poverty-stricken churches in Jerusalem (2 Cor. 9:5; cf. Rom. 15:25–26). When we hear that other churches have experienced natural disasters, famine, or loss of resources, we ought to overflow "in a wealth of generosity" (2 Cor. 8:2) toward their congregations. By giving, we sacrifice our own church's comfort in order to help Christ's suffering people, affirming that we are one in Christ. In this act, we conform to the image of Christ our head, who "though he was rich" yet for the sake of the church "became poor" (2 Cor. 8:9).

We also read about another kind of cross-church contribution in the New Testament. Frequently, local churches willingly gave up workers from their churches to serve the needs of other congregations. In the book of Acts, Barnabas brought Saul (later, Paul) from Tarsus to Antioch because the newborn church in Antioch needed help, and "for a whole year they met with the church and taught a great many people" (11:26). Later, Paul sent Timothy from Corinth to Thessalonica to help the struggling church by ministering the word to them for a period of time (1 Thess. 3:2). At times, we too may send some of our members to a newly planted church that needs mature believers; we may send our elders to assist a church without shepherds; we may send our pastor to preach to a congregation that does not have one. These corporate self-denials are not in vain. As the writer to the Hebrews reminds us, "Do not neglect to do good and to share what you have, for such sacrifices are pleasing to God" (Heb. 13:16).

4. Recommendation

Six months ago, when a nearby Baptist church closed its doors, its members became spiritually homeless. Though our two churches obviously had some differences, our unity in vital matters of theology, combined with a scarcity of other gospel-preaching churches in the area, meant that many of the members began to worship with us. Several weeks after that church's last worship service, their pastor visited our church. While he and I stood together in the pew after the benediction, his eyes wandered around the assembly. As he spotted former members, he told me a few basic things about them and then tenderly encouraged me to get to know them, to seek opportunities for their gifts, and to delight in their loveliness. This beloved elder who had worked and worshiped alongside these people for years, shepherding their souls in both trouble and joy, now commended them to the care of our church. Even after ceasing to be a pastor, he earnestly sought the good of the flock once under his care and the good of the flock to which they now belonged.

We find similar examples of recommendation in the New Testament. Whether members are traveling from one church to another for a season or a lifetime, they take with them the testimony of their local church. The church in Ephesus bid farewell to Apollos and "wrote to the disciples to welcome him" in Achaia (Acts 18:27). Paul likewise commended Phoebe to the church at Rome (Rom. 16:1–2), Titus and an unnamed brother to the church at Corinth (2 Cor. 8:16–18), and Timothy to the church at Philippi (Phil. 2:19–20). Negatively, he publicly cautioned Timothy about Alexander the coppersmith's dangerous gospel opposition (2 Tim. 4:14–15). This was neither gossip nor slander; it was a carefully worded warning designed to protect the precious flock of God from wolfish wanderers. In our churches, members ought to seek the recommendation of the elders when they move from one church to another. By sending an official letter, the local church attests to the members' good standing in the church and commends them to the ministry of the next church. These commendations allow departing members to leave in peace and direct them to a true church for the future good of their souls.[8] They also give receiving churches confidence in welcoming these new members to their fellowship. More informally, churches can also recommend traveling gospel workers and other saints who may need hospitality or financial support. Having been welcomed ourselves by Christ, we gladly welcome one another and seek to ensure that fellow Christians receive a welcome wherever they go (cf. Rom. 15:7).

5. Consultation and Admonition

Churches also need accountability to other churches, and, historically, such mutual oversight has been a widely accepted practice.[9] Typically this oversight takes place at interchurch elders' meetings, where the gathered men discuss common concerns and make decisions that promote the good of the local churches. An assembly of elders from multiple churches may not seem exciting, but it is God's kind gift to protect churches against false teaching, unresolved conflict, corporate sin, and theological error. Not long after Christ's ascension, the local churches in Antioch found themselves in trouble, and that's why one of the earliest events in the New Testament church was an interchurch elders' meeting.

In Acts 15 we read that a corruption of the gospel threatened the well-being of the churches: Judean preachers were insisting that circumcision was necessary for salvation (15:1). At first, Paul and Silas attempted to address the situation themselves (15:2) but soon realized they needed help. Gathering in Jerusalem with other "apostles and elders" (15:6) who "were appointed" (15:2) as representatives of the various churches, this council of elders held a meeting. They discussed the issue in light of the Scriptures, came to a conclusion (circumcision is *not* necessary for salvation), and sent a letter to the churches to explain their decision (15:6–32).

As the local church, it may be costly to send your elders to such meetings. You may have to give up time they could have spent working in your midst or pay for their travel to a meeting site. You may not even see any obvious fruit from their attendance. But sending your elders to these assemblies is an important investment in the health of the wider church. You can support your elders—and pray for them—in this connection to other churches because this is one of God's means of protecting the peace and purity of your own congregation and the congregations with whom you share fellowship.

A Great Multitude

The local church is part of a multitude in this world, and it will be part of an even greater multitude in the new heavens and the new earth. When the traveling Israelites sang about the joy of gathering with all the tribes (Ps. 122:4), they were singing about the physical temple in Old Testament Jerusalem. But they were also singing about heaven. In the book of Revelation, God draws back the curtain of eternity and allows us to see the reality of things to come. We read:

> I [John] saw the holy city, new Jerusalem, coming down out of heaven from God, prepared as a bride adorned for her husband. And I heard a loud voice from the throne saying, "Behold the dwelling place of God is with man. He will dwell with them, and they will be his people, and God himself with be with them as their God." (Rev. 21:2–3)

And also, "Behold, a great multitude that no one could number, from every nation, from all tribes and peoples and languages, standing before the throne and before the Lamb . . ."

(Rev. 7:9). One day soon, because of the work of Christ, all of God's people will be gathered with him forever.

Over the course of this book, we have seen glorious realities about the ordinary churches to which we belong. We have seen that these otherwise unremarkable congregations are beloved of the triune God from all eternity. In the assembly of his people, Christ makes himself known and fills us with his fullness. In the assembly of his people, Christ shepherds our souls. The people of our churches are precious to him—his holy ones, his brothers and sisters, his fellow workers. And the worship we offer is the worship he commands, leads, perfects, and tenderly accepts. In the unassuming gathering of the local church, we fellowship with Christ himself. Dear Christian, we have no greater privilege. In this life, however, these are sometimes veiled realities. Our churches continue to appear insignificant, our members continue to be weak and flawed, our worship continues to be imperfect and half-hearted, our fellowship continues to be plagued by selfishness and indifference. But the testimony of Scripture is clear: Christ is even now making his church lovely, and one day it will be absolutely perfect.

In eternity the scattered people of God from all ages and places will finally be gathered. Our real spiritual connection will be made completely visible, and we will live together in the same time and space. On that day, the local church will cease to exist. In its place will be a single congregation of all the redeemed. And we will worship. The praise that we sing so feebly now in our own congregations will become the thunderous shout of all God's people. The words of God that are preached to us now in human weakness will be declared to us by the Word himself. The sacraments that we now receive to signify Christ and his benefits will pass away, and, washed perfectly holy in his blood, we will feast with him at his everlasting table. The men and women and children of our local churches who now seem so very ordinary will be transformed—made like Christ himself. And we will be together with the Lord.

Dear member of Christ's church, soon you will hear the voice of Christ calling you: "Come up" (Rev. 4:1). Come up to the heavenly Jerusalem. Come up to the city with foundations. Come up to the very throne of God and the near presence of Christ. Come up to the assembly of the redeemed. Come, join the multitude.

This vision of the local church's sure and certain future ought to encourage our hearts. Soon, the ordinary congregations to which we belong will be glorified, and it is right for us to eagerly anticipate that day. But, in that day, your church will be no more precious to Christ than it is today. The church in eternity will appear more lovely, but it will not be more loved. And as we commit ourselves even now to the local church, we testify to this reality. Because Christ delights in the church, we delight in it. Because Christ calls it his own, we call it our own. Because Christ loves the church, we love it too. Week after week, we give ourselves for the good of the people whom God loves. And in eternity we will not be disappointed.

Come. This is where you belong.

Acknowledgments

Thanks be to God:

For the local churches to which I have had the immense privilege of belonging. The congregations of West Springfield Covenant Community Church, Pinehaven Presbyterian Church, First Presbyterian Church, Hillcrest Presbyterian Church, and the Presbyterian Church of Coventry have been my people. They'd be first to tell you that they are pretty ordinary. I'll be the first to tell you that in their company I have known the fellowship of Christ.

For Rob, who is my husband, brother, and shepherd. His love for the church kindles my own.

For my parents, Brad and Patsy Evans, who taught me from childhood that a life lived in the local church is a good life. They were not wrong.

For Nathan and Kathy Lee, Lindsey Carlson, Charlie Wingard, Dad, and Rob, who wielded their red pens so that you might be better served by these pages. It is a fearful thing to rightly divide the truth of God's word; I'm glad I didn't have to do it alone.

For the entire team at Crossway who worked cheerfully and tirelessly to bring this book to print, and especially for Dave DeWit, who championed my idea; Lydia Brownback, who tightened my sentences; and Lauren Susanto and Amy

Kruis, who promoted the book to readers. Over the years, these kingdom servants have become friends. I am grateful.

And for the multitude of God's people who helped me by prayer.

Study Questions

Introduction

Think back over your experiences in the local church. What aspects of the church are particularly precious to you? Why? How have you seen spiritual fruit in your life as a result of belonging to the local church?

Chapter 1: Beloved

Getting Started. When was the first time you realized you had a people in the local church? Is this something you think about often? Why or why not?

1. For how long has God loved his people (see Jer. 31:3)? How does he reveal his love in creation, in his dealings with Israel, at the cross, and in local churches since Christ's ascension?
2. We noted that God loves the unlovely. How does the unbiased (or "uncaused") character of God's love for us shape our attitudes toward awkward and frustrating people in the local church?
3. God loves us sacrificially. Read 1 John 4:9–10. How is God's love displayed? Did we love God first or did he love us first? Why is this significant when we think about loving people in our church?

4. God's love makes us lovely. What does Ephesians 5:27 say is the ultimate result of God's love for his church? In what sense does our love for other Christians make them lovely?

5. Sometimes people choose to separate themselves from the local church. How have you noticed this in your church experiences? How would you use God's love for his people to encourage someone who thinks the church is optional?

Further Study. Read John 17.

- How does the timing and context of this prayer reveal Christ's love for his church?
- Make a list of the petitions Jesus asks the Father to grant his people.
- Two common themes of this prayer are unity and love. Note the verses where Jesus talks about unity and love between the Father and the Son. Note the verses where he talks about unity and love among Christians. How are unity and love related? How does Trinitarian unity and love inform and encourage our human love?
- Take a minute to pray that God would grant the members of your local church unity and mutual love. Be encouraged that this is also Christ's desire; you are asking the Father for the same things that the Son is asking!

Chapter 2: Called

Getting Started. Are there people in your church with whom you have an immediate, natural affinity? What is the basis for your connection? Are there people in your local church you have difficulty relating to? Why do you think this is?

1. What is your Christian testimony? How is it different from the testimonies of other people in your

church? If you are doing these questions in a group setting, ask everyone to share a brief version of their testimony.

2. Reread Ephesians 2:1–3. Make a list of the descriptive words and phrases that define men and women apart from God. How does it encourage us to know that everyone in the church has the same past?

3. At first glance, our day-to-day life can seem quite different from the lives of the people in the church. Why is the deeper reality of Ephesians 2:4–6 important to recognize?

4. If our testimony is the same as others in our church in life, it will also be the same in death. Which older Christians have set you an example of faith to the end? Read Hebrews 11.

5. Sometimes people will distance themselves from the local church because they don't feel like they have much in common with the people there. How have you noticed this in your church experiences? How would you use the truth of our shared/mutual calling to encourage someone who feels this way?

Further Study. Read Psalm 136.

- What do the Israelites praise God for in verses 4–9? What do they praise him for in verses 10–16? In verses 17–22?

- What is the refrain after every verse? Imagine what it would have been like to sing this with all of God's people at the dedication of Solomon's temple (2 Chron. 7:3). Imagine what it will be like to sing about our testimony with the multitude in heaven (Rev. 5:11–14).

- Reread verses 23–26. How is each of those verses true for you and for all the members of your church? What was your "low estate"? Who were your "foes"? How does the Lord give food to you, supplying all your needs?

- What songs does your church sing that affirm your common testimony? Why is it important to praise God together for our salvation?

Chapter 3: Church

Getting Started. Do you have a usual seat in church? Do other people? Where do you prefer to sit, and why?

1. What does the Bible typically mean by *ekklesia*? Can you think of several examples of God's people gathering for worship in both the Old and New Testaments?
2. Why is it significant that Jesus prioritized corporate worship during his earthly life? How does it encourage you when worship in your local church seems imperfect?
3. Look at the list of biblical worship elements on page 50. Can you think of New Testament examples of the church doing each of those things in corporate worship?
4. In this chapter, we noted that the church at worship is a colony or outpost of heaven. In what sense is our local congregation on Sunday part of the unceasing worship in heaven?
5. Sometimes people believe they are closer to God alone than when they are in church worship. How have you noticed this in your church experiences? How could you use the glorious truth about corporate worship to encourage someone who thinks this way?

Further Study. Read Revelation 19:1–9.

- What groups of people are mentioned in this text (vv. 1, 4, 6)? What are they doing?

- Whose is the voice "from the throne" (v. 5)? What is he calling the people to do? In what sense is Jesus our worship leader even in the local church?
- What is the theme of the multitude's songs (vv. 1–2, 6–8)?
- Notice that in this glimpse of a heavenly "worship service," the people speak to God and God speaks to them. In your local church, which parts of your worship service are the congregation speaking to God? Which parts are God speaking to the people? Which are both?

Chapter 4: Flock

Getting Started. Have you ever wondered what your pastor does on a Tuesday afternoon or a Friday morning? In addition to their public ministry (preaching and teaching), what things have you noticed the elders of your church doing to care for the congregation?

1. On pages 62–63, we noted that in order to fully receive the shepherding of the elders, we must first identify as the flock. What other biblical examples of God's people being named and counted can you think of? What are the important benefits of church membership?
2. Reread the list of diagnostic questions for sheep on page 64. How willingly do you submit to your elders as they shepherd? Which areas come easily to you? Which areas need improvement?
3. What do you know about sheep? How does thinking of yourself as a sheep in a flock shape your view of yourself and your needs?
4. What do you know about shepherds? How does this image and the other images we explored in this chapter

shape your view of your otherwise ordinary-looking elders?

5. Sometimes people think they don't need the pastoral care of church elders. How have you seen this in your church experiences? What would you say about the goodness of being shepherded to encourage someone who thinks this way?

Further Study. Read Psalm 23.

• Make a list of the good things the shepherd provides for the sheep.

• What is the situation in verse 4? What does that teach us about our lifelong need for shepherding?

• Why is it sometimes necessary for a shepherd to use unpleasant measures ("rod" and "staff," v. 4) for the good of the sheep? Compare this image with Hebrews 12:5–12.

• Look at verses 5–6. How does the care of a shepherd yield lasting—even everlasting—blessing in the lives of the flock? How does the care of your elders yield blessing in your life? Be specific.

Chapter 5: Body

Getting Started. Where is your church's interconnectedness revealed? Do people linger after a worship service or talk during a coffee break? What is encouraging about that time? What is sometimes discouraging? What are you usually doing during that time?

1. On page 76 we learned that "God's unified people are evidence of his blessing; God's scattered people are evidence of his judgment." How was this true in the

148

Old Testament? How was it true in the New Testament? How has it been true in your own church experience?

2. In what ways is the local church like a physical human body? List the three characteristics of the church as a body that we noted from 1 Corinthians 12 (see pp. 77–79).

3. Have you ever felt that your church didn't have the right people with the right gifts? Have you ever felt like a misfit in your church? Read 1 Corinthians 12:18, 24. How do these verses encourage you and give you confidence?

4. How do we experience the fullness of Christ in the church? Why is it impossible to experience this fullness on our own, as individuals?

5. Sometimes people think their gifts are not necessary in the local church or that the local church is not necessary for the exercise of their gifts. How have you noticed this in your church experience? What would you say about the beautifully arranged body of Christ to encourage someone who thinks this way?

Further Study. Read Nehemiah 3.

- List some of the tasks and the people who completed them. Notice how many specific details this chapter of Nehemiah gives us.
- Read verse 12. Who is doing the repair work? What is surprising about this? How does this verse point ahead to the truth of Galatians 3:28?
- Look at verse 5. What is sad about these verses? How is the attitude of the "nobles" of Tekoa described? Think of a situation in the church where you have had the same attitude.

- What lessons can we draw from this description of the work on the wall? How can we apply this to our life in the local church?

Chapter 6: Saints

Getting Started. When you hear the word *saint*, what comes to mind? What characteristics do you think saints possess? Do you ever think of your local church as the saints? Why or why not?

1. Do you tend to think of yourself as being holy or as becoming holy? How are both of these things true at the same time?
2. How do we know that holiness was important for the Old Testament people of God? How do we know it is important for the church in this age?
3. We saw five ways the local church contributes to our holiness. Which of those ways was most familiar to you? Which, if any, was new? Identify one way you want to more intentionally invest in the holiness of your local church.
4. The state of the church's holiness can be discouraging at times. In what ways is the church sometimes less holy than it ought to be? Why is the perfect holiness of Christ an encouragement to us when the saints don't seem very holy?
5. Sometimes people—even people in the church—think they don't need church to be holy. How have you seen this? What would you say about the community project of holiness to encourage someone who thinks this way?

Further Study. Read Exodus 20.

- Who were the commandments given to? (See Deut. 5:1–5.) How does the fact that they were given to the whole congregation change the way we understand them?

- Read verse 2. What is the reason that God's people should obey these commandments? How is their identity, and the identity of their God, tied to obedience in other places in the commandments?
- What are some specific ways the local church helps you to obey the commandments?
- How are these commandments a picture of Christ? List some specific examples from the life of Christ that demonstrate his perfect conformity to the law of God. How does Christ's obedience to the commandments encourage the local church, his body?

Chapter 7: Brothers and Sisters

Getting Started. Do you use the terms *brother* and *sister* for the people in your local church? Have you been in other churches that do? When you hear those terms, how does it affect your perception of the men and women around you?

1. On page 102 we noted that "throughout the Old Testament, having a family indicates blessing. Spouses, children, and grandchildren are clear signs of God's favor, while the lack of family—being barren, orphaned, or widowed—is cause for deep lament." How does the Old Testament affirmation of the blessing of biological family look slightly different when we come to the New Testament?
2. In what ways is Christ's family similar to a biological family? In what ways is it different? How do the Epistles inform our understanding of spiritual family life?
3. What does a holy kiss look like in the context of your local church? Give some examples of culturally appropriate, morally chaste, physical expressions of love that you can begin (or continue) to practice.

4. Read Hebrews 2:10–13. Why is it striking that Christ is "not ashamed to call them brothers" (v. 11)? How can his example be an encouragement to you in your local church? How is Christ our ultimate source of joy as we share family life with our Christian brothers and sisters?

5. Sometimes people who attend church admit to not actually liking their fellow church members very much. How have you seen this? What would you say about being brothers and sisters to encourage someone who feels this way?

Further Study. Read Romans 16.

• List the names given in this passage. Note the unique details about many of the church members. What does this careful attention tell us about Paul's love for the members of the Roman church?

• What does Paul call Phoebe (v. 1), Rufus's mother (v. 13), Asyncritus's companions (v. 14), and Quartus (v. 23)? Do you regularly think of—and speak of—your fellow church members as your family? How could you cultivate this practice in your life?

• What does Paul call the Christians in the beginning of verse 17? How does this declaration of their family relationship relate to the instructions that follow in verses 17–20?

• Read Romans 1:8–15. What desire does Paul express four times in this text (vv. 10, 11, 13, 15)? Do you have the same desire to be physically present with God's people? Why is physical presence important (cf. Rom. 16:16)?

Chapter 8: Gospel Partners

Getting Started. What kind of work do you do? Do you have to cooperate with other people to accomplish your assigned tasks? What tasks in the local church require similar levels of teamwork?

1. How does the Great Commission (Matt. 28:18–20) incorporate elements of *going out* and of *coming in*? How does your local church fulfill Jesus's commission in those two ways?
2. On page 119 we noted five individuals and families that Paul calls his fellow workers. List those names. Which of those might we expect to see on the list? Which are surprising, and why?
3. What are the three ways the Philippian church entered into gospel partnership with Paul? How does your local church partner with gospel laborers in each of these ways?
4. Gospel partners share the labor of gospel work, and they also share its reward. How does Paul describe this reward in Philippians 1:7? In what ways have you experienced this reward in your own life and the life of your local church?
5. Sometimes people assume that all the important gospel work is done by pastors and missionaries. How have you heard this expressed? What would you say about the privilege of being gospel partners to encourage someone who thinks this way?

Further Study. Read Acts 18.

- Who were Priscilla and Aquila (vv. 2–3)? How did they help Paul (vv. 3, 18)? Who was Apollos (vv. 24–25)? How did Priscilla and Aquila help him (v. 26)?

- Read Romans 16:3–5; 1 Corinthians 16:19; and 2 Timothy 4:19. What else do we learn about Priscilla (Prisca) and Aquila in these passages?
- Paul calls Priscilla (Prisca) and Aquila his "fellow workers" (Rom. 16:3). According to Acts 18:3, they were his fellow workers in two senses. Which does Paul have in mind here? What does this term say about the value Paul placed on faithfulness, discipleship, and hospitality?
- How can Priscilla and Aquila's example encourage you as you seek to labor in the local church for the cause of Christ in the world?

Chapter 9: Multitude

Getting Started. How large is your local church? Have you ever been to a worship service that was much larger than your typical Sunday gathering (maybe at a conference or other special event)? What aspects of worshiping with that multitude gave you a small taste of heaven?

1. Reread the paragraph on page 129 beginning with "Although connections between . . ." How does the relationship between Old Testament tribes foreshadow cooperation and mutual love between New Testament local churches?
2. Read Acts 9:31. In what sense is this verse describing churches? In what sense is it describing *the* church?
3. What are the five ways that local churches express and nurture their relationship with other churches? How does your own church practice these things?
4. Read Proverbs 14:28 (also see p. 128) and 2 Corinthians 8:23. How is Jesus's glory connected to the multitude in heaven?

5. Sometimes people believe (or act like) their local church functions perfectly well without a relationship to other churches. How have you seen this? What would you say about the vision of a multitude to encourage someone who thinks or acts this way?

Further Study. Read Psalm 122.

- As the Israelites began this song, what desire did they express (v. 1)? What practical action did they take (v. 2)?
- What aspects of worship in Jerusalem delight the singers? In what sense is this a meditation on the earthly Jerusalem? In what sense is it a meditation on the heavenly one?
- What do the singers pray and work toward (vv. 6–9)? How can we apply this to our local churches?
- Do you regularly meditate on the prospect of worshiping with the multitude in eternity? Do you sing about it? Do you pray for it? Do you look eagerly toward that day?

Notes

Introduction

1. Herman Witsius, *Sacred Dissertations on the Apostles' Creed*, vol. 2 (repr., Grand Rapids, MI: Reformation Heritage, 2010), 370.
2. D. Martyn Lloyd-Jones, *Christian Unity* (Grand Rapids, MI: Baker, 1980), 209.
3. "In the fellowship of the Church, and within the magic circle of its influences, the believer is in a more eminent sense a believer, than apart from them." James Bannerman, *The Church of Christ: A Treatise on the Nature, Powers, Ordinances, Discipline and Government of the Christian Church*, vol. 1 (1868; repr., Birmingham, AL: Solid Ground, 2009), 92.

Chapter 1: Beloved

1. E.g., Rom. 12:19; 1 Cor. 4:14; 10:14; 15:58; 2 Cor. 7:1; 12:19; Eph. 5:1; Phil. 2:12; Col. 3:12; 2 Thess. 2:13; Heb. 6:9; James 1:19; 2:5; 1 Pet. 2:11; 4:12; 2 Pet. 3:1, 8, 17; 1 John 2:7; 3:2, 21; 4:1, 7, 11; 3 John 2, 5, 11; Jude 1, 3, 17, 20.
2. Theologians distinguish between the "invisible church" (true believers throughout all time) and the "visible church" (the church presently manifest in the world.) But though there may be some people in the visible church who are not actually believers and thus not part of the invisible church, and though the glory that belongs to the invisible church is sometimes obscured in the ordinary and imperfect visible church, we can still have confidence that when we belong to a gospel-proclaiming, sacrament-administering, biblically worshiping local church, we truly belong to the church of Christ. See, e.g., Westminster Confession of Faith in *The Confession of Faith Together with the Larger Catechism and the Shorter Catechism with Scripture Proofs*, 3rd ed. (Lawrenceville, GA: Christian Education & Publications, 1990), 25.1, 2, 4.
3. Michael Reeves, *Delighting in the Trinity: An Introduction to the Christian Faith* (Downers Grove, IL: IVP Academic, 2012), 42.

4. "What is a covenant? A relationship that God establishes with us and guarantees by his Word." *First Catechism: Teaching Children Bible Truths* (Suwanee, GA: Great Commission Publications, 2003), Q&A 24.

5. See Acts 2:39: "For the promise is for you and for your children and for all who are far off, everyone whom the Lord our God calls to himself."

6. E.g., John 13:34; 15:12, 17; Rom. 12:10; 13:8; Gal. 5:13; Eph. 4:2; 1 Thess. 3:12; 4:9; Heb. 10:24; 1 Pet. 1:22; 4:8; 1 John 3:11, 14, 16, 23; 4:7, 11, 12; 2 John 5.

7. Donald McLeod, *Christ Crucified: Understanding the Atonement* (Downers Grove, IL: IVP Academic, 2014), 134.

8. Arthur W. Pink, *The Attributes of God* (repr., Grand Rapids, MI: Baker, 1979), 77.

9. See McLeod, *Christ Crucified*, 142.

10. J. I. Packer, *Knowing God* (1973; repr., Downers Grove, IL: IVP, 1993), 126–27.

11. John R. W. Stott, *The Epistles of John: An Introduction and Commentary*, Tyndale New Testament Commentaries, ed. Leon Morris (1964; repr., Grand Rapids, MI: Eerdmans, 1988), 166.

12. Garry J. Williams, *His Love Endures Forever* (Wheaton, IL: Crossway, 2016), 179.

13. Jeremy Walker, *Life in Christ: Becoming and Being a Disciple of the Lord Jesus Christ* (Grand Rapids, MI: Reformation Heritage, 2013), 104.

14. D. A. Carson, *The Gospel according to John*, Pillar New Testament Commentary (Grand Rapids, MI: Eerdmans, 1991), 570–71.

Chapter 2: Called

1. I first told parts of the church ladies' story in this article: "The Casserole-Toting Church Ladies Hold the Secret to Happiness," *Christianity Today*, August 1, 2016, accessed July 22, 2019, https://www.christianitytoday.com/women/2016/july/casserole-toting-church-ladies-hold-secret-to-happiness.html. Used here by permission.

2. Westminster Shorter Catechism, in *The Confession of Faith Together with the Larger Catechism and the Shorter Catechism with Scripture Proofs*, 3rd ed. (Lawrenceville, GA: Christian Education & Publications, 1990), Q&A 31.

3. Richard D. Phillips, *Saved by Grace: The Glory of Salvation in Ephesians 2* (Phillipsburg, NJ: P&R, 2009), 63.

4. Westminster Shorter Catechism, Q. 88.

Chapter 3: Church

1. John Charles Bennett, "The English Anglican Practice of Pew Renting, 1800–1960," DPhil. thesis (University of Birmingham, n.d.),

24–26, accessed July 22, 2019, http://etheses.bham.ac.uk/2864/1
/Bennett_11_PhD.pdf.

2. Charles D. Cashdollar, *A Spiritual Home: Life in British and American Reformed Congregations, 1830–1915* (University Park, PA: Pennsylvania State University Press, 2000), 166–67.

3. Cited in Bennett, "The English Anglican," 219.

4. James Bannerman, *The Church of Christ: A Treatise on the Nature, Powers, Ordinances, Discipline and Government of the Christian Church*, vol. 1 (1868; repr., Vestavia Hills, AL: Solid Ground, 2009), 5–6.

5. Bannerman, *The Church of Christ*, 11.

6. Edmund P. Clowney, "Corporate Worship: A Means of Grace," in *Give Praise to God: A Vision for Reforming Worship, Celebrating the Legacy of James Montgomery Boice*, ed. Philip Graham Ryken, Derek W. H. Thomas, and J. Ligon Duncan III (Phillipsburg, NJ: P&R, 2003), 99.

7. David Clarkson, "Public Worship to Be Preferred Before Private," in *The Practical Works of David Clarkson*, vol. 3 (Edinburgh: James Nichol, 1865), 187.

8. Calvin wrote that King Jesus is "the sole lawgiver of his own worship." John Calvin, *Institutes of the Christian Religion*, ed. John T. MacNeill, trans. Ford Lewis Battles (Philadelphia: Westminster Press, 1960), 4.10.23.

9. Westminster Confession of Faith, in *The Confession of Faith Together with the Larger Catechism and the Shorter Catechism with Scripture Proofs*, 3rd ed. (Lawrenceville, GA: Christian Education & Publications, 1990), 21.1.

10. Ibid., 21.4, 5.

11. Matthew Henry, *Matthew Henry's Commentary*, vol. 6, *Acts to Revelation* (1710; repr., Peabody, MA: Hendrickson, 1991), 772.

12. Jeremiah Burroughs, cited in Joel R. Beeke, "The Beautiful, Biblical Worship of Christ's Bride: A Puritan View," in *The Beauty and Glory of Christ's Bride*, ed. Joel R. Beeke (Grand Rapids, MI: Reformation Heritage, 2015), 83.

Chapter 4: Flock

1. Timothy Z. Witmer, *The Shepherd Leader: Achieving Effective Shepherding in Your Church* (Phillipsburg, NJ: P&R, 2010), 29–30.

2. Witmer, *Shepherd Leader*, 13.

3. Elders whose primary work is teaching and preaching and who are often paid by the church for their labors (sometimes called "pastors") have a slightly different role in the local church. The Bible itself acknowledges different functions in the eldership (see 1 Tim. 5:17),

but it's beyond the scope of this chapter to make a thorough study of biblical church polity.
4. Edmund P. Clowney also makes this point in *The Church*, Contours of Christian Theology, ed. Gerald Bray (Downers Grove, IL: Inter-Varsity Press, 1995), 104.
5. Also, Paul assumes church membership when he instructs the Corinthian church to expel certain rebellious men (1 Cor. 5:9–13).
6. We'll discuss this further in chap. 9.
7. Witmer, *Shepherd Leader*.
8. Guy Prentiss Waters, *How Jesus Runs the Church* (Phillipsburg, NJ: P&R, 2011), *xxiv*.

Chapter 5: Body
1. See Rom. 12:4–8; 1 Cor. 12; Eph. 2:11–22; 4:1–16; Col. 2:8–15; 3:12–17; Heb. 13:3.
2. "All saints . . . have communion in each other's gifts and graces, and are obliged to the performance of such duties, public and private, as do conduce to their mutual good, both in the inward and outward man." Westminster Confession of Faith, in *The Confession of Faith Together with the Larger Catechism and the Shorter Catechism with Scripture Proofs*, 3rd ed. (Lawrenceville, GA: Christian Education and Publications, 1990), 26.2.
3. Roger Ellsworth, *Strengthening Christ's Church: The Message of 1 Corinthians* (Durham, UK: Evangelical Press, 1995), 205. See also, Leon Morris, *1 Corinthians*, Tyndale New Testament Commentaries, rev. ed. (Grand Rapids, MI: Eerdmans, 1993), 167.
4. Morris, *1 Corinthians*, 163.
5. Matthew Henry, *Matthew Henry's Commentary*, vol. 5, *Matthew to John* (1710; repr., Peabody, MA: Hendrickson, 1991), 723.
6. Matthew Henry, *Matthew Henry's Commentary*, vol. 6, *Acts to Revelation* (1710; repr., Peabody, MA: Hendrickson, 1991), 556.
7. Henry, *Matthew Henry's Commentary*, vol. 6, *Acts to Revelation*, 556.

Chapter 6: Saints
1. Tim Challies, "Sanctification Is a Community Project," *Challies.com*, Aug. 20, 2012, accessed July 22, 2019, http://www.challies.com/christian-living/sanctification-is-a-community-project.
2. John Murray, "The Agency in Definitive Sanctification," in *Collected Writings of John Murray*, vol. 2, *Select Lectures in Systematic Theology* (1977; repr., Carlisle, PA: Banner of Truth, 1996), 293.
3. John Murray, "Progressive Sanctification," in *Select Lectures in Systematic Theology*, 298.
4. Michael Kruger, "Saint or Sinner? Rethinking the Language of Our Christian Identity," *Canon Fodder*, July 15, 2013, https://www

.michaeljkruger.com/saint-or-sinner-rethinking-the-language-of-our
-christian-identity/.

5. Philip Graham Ryken, ed., *The Communion of the Saints: Living in Fellowship with the People of God* (Phillipsburg, NJ: P&R, 2001), 6.
6. D. Martyn Lloyd-Jones, *Christian Unity: An Exposition of Ephesians 4:1–16* (1980; repr., Grand Rapids, MI: Baker, 2003), 212. Also, Charles Hodge, *Ephesians* (1858; repr., Carlisle, PA: Banner of Truth, 2003), 172; emphasis added.
7. John R. W. Stott, *The Message of Ephesians: God's New Society* (Downers Grove, IL: InterVarsity Press, 1979), 172.
8. Christopher Ash, *Discovering the Joy of a Clear Conscience* (Phillipsburg, NJ: P&R, 2012), 157.
9. Hodge, *Ephesians*, 167.
10. F. F. Bruce, cited in P. T. O'Brien, *The Letter to the Ephesians* (Grand Rapids, MI: Eerdmans, 1999), 308.
11. Lloyd-Jones, *Christian Unity*, 212.
12. Lloyd-Jones, *Christian Unity*, 199.

Chapter 7: Brothers and Sisters

1. Colin Brown, ed., *The New International Dictionary of New Testament Theology* (1967; repr., Grand Rapids, MI: Zondervan, 1989), s.v. "Brother, Neighbor, Friend."
2. I use *biological* in a broad sense to mean "natural" or "human," as opposed to "spiritual." As the mother of two children by birth and two by adoption, I am daily thankful that God sometimes forms families out of people with no genetic relationship to one another, and I do not intend to discount this by my language.
3. See Daniel M. Doriani, *Matthew*, vol. 1, *Chapters 1–13*, Reformed Expository Commentary, ed. Richard D. Phillips and Philip G. Ryken (Phillipsburg, NJ: P&R, 2008), 538.
4. Dietrich Bonhoeffer, *Life Together* (1954; repr., New York: Harper & Row, 1976), 30.
5. Rom. 1:9–15; 15:23–24; 1 Cor. 16:7; Phil. 2:23–24; 1 Thess. 2:17; 3:10; 2 Tim. 1:4.
6. A few sentences in the previous two paragraphs are adapted from my article: "Bring Back the Holy Kiss," The Gospel Coalition, July 31, 2014, accessed July 22, 2019, https://www.thegospelcoalition.org/article/bring-back-the-holy-kiss/.
7. Jeremy Walker, *Life in Christ: Becoming and Being a Disciple of the Lord Jesus Christ* (Grand Rapids, MI: Reformation Heritage, 2013), 104–5.

Chapter 8: Gospel Partners

1. For a helpful discussion of the church's mission and how it relates to questions of social justice, see Kevin DeYoung and Greg Gilbert,

What Is the Mission of the Church? Making Sense of Social Justice, Shalom, and the Great Commission (Wheaton, IL: Crossway, 2011).

2. Christopher J. H. Wright, *The Mission of God: Unlocking the Bible's Grand Narrative* (Downers Grove, IL: IVP Academic, 2006), 194–95.
3. Wright, *The Mission of God*, 478.
4. Creighton Marlowe, cited in Wright, *The Mission of God*, 484.
5. See Wright, *The Mission of God*, 523–24.
6. D. A. Carson, *Basics for Believers: An Exposition of Philippians* (Grand Rapids, MI: Baker Academic, 1996), 16–17.
7. William Hendriksen, *Exposition of Philippians*, New Testament Commentary (1962; repr., Grand Rapids, MI: Baker, 1979), 53.
8. Carson, *Basics for Believers*, 55.
9. I more fully explore the duty and delight of corporate prayer in *Praying Together: The Priority and Privilege of Prayer in Our Homes, Communities, and Churches* (Wheaton, IL: Crossway, 2016).
10. Matthew Henry, *Matthew Henry's Commentary*, vol. 6, *Acts to Revelation* (1710; repr., Peabody, MA: Hendrickson, 1991), 584.

Chapter 9: Multitude

1. Barna Group, "The Most Post-Christian Cities in America: 2019," *Barna*, June 5, 2019, accessed July 22, 2019, https://www.barna.com /research/post-christian-cities-2019/.
2. *The Cambridge Platform of Church Discipline Adopted in 1648 and the Confession of Faith Adopted in 1680* (repr., Boston: Perkins & Whipple, 1850), 77.
3. I am indebted to my twelve-year-old son Brad for making this point while I was discussing this chapter at lunch one Sunday.
4. Guy Waters, *How Jesus Runs the Church* (Phillipsburg, NJ: P&R, 2011), 121.
5. Waters, *How Jesus Runs the Church*, 120.
6. I believe Presbyterian church government—which makes the communion of churches formal and binding—is the most biblical expression of interchurch relations. For a helpful explanation of Presbyterian polity and its biblical justification, see Waters, *How Jesus Runs the Church*.
7. I am indebted to a Baptist pastor, David Chanski, for significantly shaping my thinking on this subject through his material in two conference addresses. Chanski, in turn, acknowledges his own indebtedness to the work of several Puritan ministers, including John Cotton, John Owen, and Thomas Goodwin. David Chanski, "Church Unity: Elements of Communion: Part 1" and "Church Unity: Elements of Communion: Part 2," conference addresses, 2015 Trinity Pastor's Conference, Trinity Baptist Church, Montville, NJ, October 19, 2015.

8. In my denomination, the Presbyterian Church in America, this is called a "letter of transfer." These letters are accepted not only by churches in the same denomination, but also more widely among churches in like-minded denominations.

9. This is intrinsic to Presbyterianism, of course, in which the elders of churches in a region meet regularly as a presbytery or classis and the elders of all the churches meet as a general assembly or synod. These bodies exercise real authority over the churches. But even congregationalism (which includes Baptist churches) has historically acknowledged the importance of nonbinding consultation and admonition between local churches. The Cambridge Platform, Savoy Declaration, and 1689 Confession—documents that prescribe congregational polity—each have sections affirming the value of receiving counsel from other churches.

Bibliography

Ash, Christopher. *Discovering the Joy of a Clear Conscience.* Phillipsburg, NJ: P&R, 2012.

Bannerman, James. *The Church of Christ: A Treatise on the Nature, Powers, Ordinances, Discipline and Government of the Christian Church.* Vol. 1. 1868. Reprint, Birmingham, AL: Solid Ground Christian Books, 2009.

Barna Group. "The Most Post-Christian Cities in America: 2019." *Barna.* June 5, 2019. https://www.barna.com/research/post-christian-cities-2019/.

Beeke, Joel R. "The Beautiful, Biblical Worship of Christ's Bride: A Puritan View." In *The Beauty and Glory of Christ's Bride,* edited by Joel R. Beeke, 81–102. Grand Rapids, MI: Reformation Heritage, 2015.

Bennett, John Charles. "The English Anglican Practice of Pew Renting, 1800–1960." DPhil thesis, University of Birmingham. N.d. http://etheses.bham.ac.uk/2864/1/Bennett_11_PhD.pdf.

Bonhoeffer, Dietrich. *Life Together.* 1954. Reprint. New York: Harper & Row, 1976.

Brown, Colin, ed. *The New International Dictionary of New Testament Theology.* Vol. 1, A–F. 1967. Reprint. Grand Rapids, MI: Zondervan, 1989.

Calvin, John. *Institutes of the Christian Religion.* Edited by John T. MacNeill. Translated by Ford Lewis Battles. Philadelphia: Westminster Press, 1960.

Cambridge Platform of Church Discipline Adopted in 1648 and the Confession of Faith Adopted in 1680, The. Reprint. Boston: Perkins & Whipple, 1850.

Carson, D. A. *Basics for Believers: An Exposition of Philippians*. Grand Rapids, MI: Baker Academic, 1996.

Carson, D. A. *The Gospel according to John*. Pillar New Testament Commentary. Grand Rapids, MI: Eerdmans, 1991.

Cashdollar, Charles D. *A Spiritual Home: Life in British and American Reformed Congregations, 1830–1915*. University Park, PA: Pennsylvania State University Press, 2000.

Challies, Tim. "Sanctification Is a Community Project." *Challies. com*. August 20, 2012. http://www.challies.com/christian -living/sanctification-is-a-community-project.

Chanski, David. "Church Unity: Elements of Communion: Part 1." Conference address, 2015 Trinity Pastor's Conference, Trinity Baptist Church, Montville, NJ, October 19, 2015.

Chanski, David. "Church Unity: Elements of Communion: Part 2." Conference address, 2015 Trinity Pastor's Conference, Trinity Baptist Church, Montville, NJ, October 19, 2015.

David Clarkson. "Public Worship to Be Preferred Before Private." In *The Practical Works of David Clarkson*. Vol. 3. Edinburgh: James Nichol, 1865.

Clowney, Edmund P. *The Church*. Contours of Christian Theology. Edited by Gerald Bray. Downers Grove, IL: InterVarsity Press, 1995.

Clowney, Edmund P. "Corporate Worship: A Means of Grace." In *Give Praise to God: A Vision for Reforming Worship, Celebrating the Legacy of James Montgomery Boice*. Edited by Philip Graham Ryken, Derek W. H. Thomas, and J. Ligon Duncan III, 94–101. Phillipsburg, NJ: P&R, 2003.

Confession of Faith Together with the Larger Catechism and the Shorter Catechism with Scripture Proofs, The. 3rd ed. Lawrenceville, GA: Christian Education & Publications, 2004.

DeYoung, Kevin, and Greg Gilbert. *What Is the Mission of the Church? Making Sense of Social Justice, Shalom, and the Great Commission*. Wheaton, IL: Crossway, 2011.

Doriani, Daniel M. *Matthew*. Vol. 1, *Chapters 1–13*. Reformed Expository Commentary. Edited by Richard D. Phillips and Philip G. Ryken. Phillipsburg, NJ: P&R, 2008.

Ellsworth, Roger. *Strengthening Christ's Church: The Message of 1 Corinthians*. Durham, UK: Evangelical Press, 1995.

First Catechism: Teaching Children Bible Truths. Suwanee, GA: Great Commission Publications, 2003.

Hendriksen, William. *Exposition of Philippians*. New Testament Commentary. 1962. Reprint, Grand Rapids, MI: Baker, 1979.

Henry, Matthew. *Matthew Henry's Commentary*. Vol. 5, *Matthew to John*. 1710. Reprint, Peabody, MA: Hendrickson, 1991.

Henry, Matthew. *Matthew Henry's Commentary*. Vol. 6, *Acts to Revelation*. 1710. Reprint, Peabody, MA: Hendrickson, 1991.

Hill, Megan. "Bring Back the Holy Kiss." The Gospel Coalition. July 31, 2014. https://www.thegospelcoalition.org/article/bring-back-the-holy-kiss/.

Hill, Megan. "The Casserole-Toting Church Ladies Hold the Secret to Happiness." *Christianity Today*. August 1, 2016. https://www.christianitytoday.com/women/2016/july/casserole-toting-church-ladies-hold-secret-to-happiness.html.

Hill, Megan. *Praying Together: The Priority and Privilege of Prayer in Our Homes, Communities, and Churches*. Wheaton, IL: Crossway, 2016.

Hodge, Charles. *Ephesians*. 1858. Reprint, Carlisle, PA: Banner of Truth, 2003.

Kruger, Michael. "Saint or Sinner? Rethinking the Language of Our Christian Identity." *Canon Fodder*. July 15, 2013. https://www.michaeljkruger.com/saint-or-sinner-rethinking-the-language-of-our-christian-identity/.

Lloyd-Jones, D. Martyn. *Christian Unity: An Exposition of Ephesians 4:1–16*. 1980. Reprint, Grand Rapids, MI: Baker Books, 2003.

McLeod, Donald. *Christ Crucified: Understanding the Atonement*. Downers Grove, IL: IVP Academic, 2014.

Morris, Leon. *1 Corinthians*. Tyndale New Testament Commentaries. Revised edition. Grand Rapids, MI: Eerdmans, 1993.

Murray, John. *Collected Writings of John Murray*. Vol. 2, *Select Lectures in Systematic Theology*. 1977. Reprint, Carlisle, PA: Banner of Truth, 1996.

O'Brien, P. T. *The Letter to the Ephesians*. Grand Rapids, MI: Eerdmans, 1999.

Packer, J. I. *Knowing God*. 1973. Reprint, Downers Grove, IL: InterVarsity Press, 1993.

Phillips, Richard D. *Saved by Grace: The Glory of Salvation in Ephesians 2*. Phillipsburg, NJ: P&R, 2009.

Pink, Arthur W. *The Attributes of God*. Reprint, Grand Rapids, MI: Baker, 1979.

Reeves, Michael. *Delighting in the Trinity: An Introduction to the Christian Faith*. Downers Grove, IL: IVP Academic, 2012.

Ryken, Philip Graham. *The Communion of the Saints: Living in Fellowship with the People of God*. Phillipsburg, NJ: P&R, 2001.

Ryken, Philip Graham, ed. *The Message of Ephesians: God's New Society*. Downers Grove, IL: InterVarsity Press, 1979.

Stott, John R. W. *The Epistles of John: An Introduction and Commentary*. Tyndale New Testament Commentaries, edited by Leon Morris. 1964. Reprint, Grand Rapids, MI: Eerdmans.

Walker, Jeremy. *Life in Christ: Becoming and Being a Disciple of the Lord Jesus Christ*. Grand Rapids, MI: Reformation Heritage, 2013.

Waters, Guy Prentiss. *How Jesus Runs the Church*. Phillipsburg, NJ: P&R, 2011.

Williams, Garry J. *His Love Endures Forever*. Wheaton, IL: Crossway, 2016.

Witmer, Timothy Z. *The Shepherd Leader: Achieving Effective Shepherding in Your Church*. Phillipsburg, NJ: P&R, 2010.

Witsius, Herman. *Sacred Dissertations on the Apostles' Creed*. Vol. 2. Reprint, Grand Rapids, MI: Reformation Heritage, 2010.

Wright, Christopher J. H. *The Mission of God: Unlocking the Bible's Grand Narrative*. Downers Grove, IL: IVP Academic, 2006.

General Index

Scripture Index

Equipping Another Generation to Practice and Delight in Prayer

Exploring the Bible's teaching on corporate prayer and the rich blessings that result, *Praying Together* will help you delight in the privilege of prayer and give you the practical tools to make praying with others a regular practice in your home, your church, and your community.

"This book will remind you of how good and pleasant it is when God's people dwell—and pray—together in unity."
KATELYN BEATY, Managing Editor, *Christianity Today*

"Megan Hill has given us a primer on prayer that is both useful and eloquent."
JEN WILKIN, Director of Classes and Curriculum, The Village Church; author, *Women of the Word*; *None Like Him*; and *In His Image*

For more information, visit **crossway.org**.